CC

GERMANS ARE FUNNY

A Guide to Teaching Foreign Languages

Not a textbook or lesson planner, but ideas and inspiration for activities in-and-outside-of-the-classroom for teaching German as a foreign language, or other foreign languages, to students grades 6 – 12.

Germans are Funny. 1st Edition (2007)
Germans are Funny. 2nd Edition (2008)
Germans are Funny. 3rd Edition (2009)
Germans are Funny. 4th Edition (2016)

© Copyright 2007 - 2016 by Conrad Rehbach

Cover design: Conrad Rehbach

Acknowledgements

Thank you, Marjorie Rehbach, for help with editing, moral support, great advice, and expert proof reading. For any spelling, grammatical, or other possible mistakes, still contained in this book, and discovered by you, the reader, please contact her.

Thank you to all my students, past and present. Your dedication to learning, and your ingenuity concerning excuses for homework not done on time, served as a constant inspiration to me.

Table of Contents

Introduction   7

1. *Das Diktat (Dictation)*   11
2. *Das Gedicht (Poetry)*   53
3. *Im Restaurant (Restaurant)*   71
4. *Das Wetter (Weather)*   83
5. *Das Rätsel (Riddles)*   95
6. *Wo bin ich? (Where am I?)*   105
7. *Bildergeschichten und Filme*
   (Stories with Pictures and Movies)   131
8. *Die Übersetzung (Translations)*   145
9. *Der Test (Tests)*   169
10. *Der Kurs (Course Announcement)*   243
11. *Die Noten (Grades)*   247
12. *Der Wochenbericht (Weekly Reports)*   253
13. *Der Semesterbericht*
   (Semester Reports)   263

Bibliography   271

About the Author   275

Germans Are Funny

Introduction

There is a wide variety of textbooks and materials available to teachers of *German as a foreign language* within the English speaking culture. Much of this material is geared towards the grade school student or the college student. In my work as a teacher of high school age students, I experienced both a certain shortage of materials meant for this age group, and also a need to draw ideas for in-and-out-of-the-classroom activities from a great variety of sources.

This book – although it might become a classic - is not a traditional textbook or workbook for students' or teachers' use, but rather a collection of exercises, ideas for classroom activities, and inspirational material for teachers to use and adapt to their own situation.

Drawn from many years of teaching German as a foreign language to Waldorf high school students (ranging from the beginners' to the advanced levels) in an alternative Waldorf high school setting that included small classes in an innovative school environment, where flexibility and love for learning were equally important, this book is a collection of classroom materials geared towards students, grades 6 to 12, in alternative schools, charter schools, Waldorf schools or homeschooling. The material presented and collected here in this book is meant to be a supplement (and possibly an inspiration) to curriculum planning, course materials, and lesson plans.

The material is grouped by activities and subjects, rather than sequentially reflecting levels of language proficiency. Most of the activities, exercises and texts can easily be adapted towards usage in classroom settings or with individual students of different levels of skills and knowledge of the German language, or other foreign languages.

Composition VIII by Wassily Kandinsky (1866 – 1944)

Karl Valentin (1882 – 1948)

Germans Are Funny

Chapter 1: *Das Diktat (Dictation)*

Dictation exercises are often looked down upon as being outdated, dull and questionable as to their benefit towards learning a foreign language. I believe dictation exercises are an essential element of learning a foreign language, and should be used more often. Once a week at least! The students learn very well this way, as they are challenged to listen attentively to each sentence, word and syllable, and have to translate the auditory information received into words and sentences that

they write down, thereby engaging their whole body in a threefold way, as the sensory information is being processed, felt, and brought down on paper via the fine motor skills necessary to write.

Students need to be able to relate to the content of the dictation. There need to be words they already know, and new ones that they need to figure out. There needs to be a story (if ever so simple) that makes some sense and is interesting in such a way that the students intellect is challenged and their feelings touched. No dry, boring, careful-not-to-offend-anyone, politically correct stories please! These are *uncool*. Many of the stories presented here have references to political figures, social situations, localities the students know, etc., and would need to be adapted and updated to your and your students' situation.

Frau von Hinterberg.

Am Donnerstag geht die schöne Frau von Hinterberg zu dem Common Ground cafe in Viroqua. Die nette Frau von Hinterberg bestellt einen heißen Kaffee und zwei Brötchen mit Marmelade und Honig. Aber der Kaffee ist zu heiß. Da schreit die liebe Frau von Hinterberg: "Der Kaffee ist fürchterlich!" Die Bedienung kommt zu Frau von Hinterberg und singt: "La, la, la, la, la, la, la, laaaaah." Frau von Hinterberg ißt das kleine Brötchen mit viel Marmelade und wenig Honig. Dann geht die süße Frau von Hinterberg nach Hause.

Mrs. von Behindthemountain.

On Thursday the beautiful Mrs. von Behindthemountain goes to the Common Ground café in Viroqua. The cute Mrs. von Behindthemountain orders a hot coffee and two rolls with jam and honey. But the coffee is too hot. Now the lovely Mrs. von Behindthemountain yells: "The coffee is horrible!" The waitress comes to Mrs. von Behindthemountain and sings: "La, la, la, la, la, la, la, laaaaah." Mrs. von Behindthemountain eats the little roll with lots of jam and little honey. Then the sweet Mrs. von Behindthemountain goes home.

Typically a dictation is given by reading each sentence out loud, repeating it twice, and if we deal with a long sentence, with pauses between parts of the sentence. Punctuation is given in German, and written on the blackboard for the first few times. It is important to really get into the story and emphasize certain words, or change the intonation appropriately, especially when reciting "wörtliche Rede." (Quotation)

Frau Müller.

Am Mittwoch geht die schöne Frau Müller zu dem kleinen Café in Rosenheim. Die nette Frau Müller bestellt einen heißen Kaffee. Die freundliche Bedienung bringt der hübschen Frau Müller Kaffee. Aber der Kaffee ist kalt. Da schreit die liebe Frau Müller: "Der Kaffee ist fürchterlich!" Die langsame Bedienung kommt zu der wilden Frau Müller und sagt: "Der Kaffee ist nicht kalt." Frau Müller ist ärgerlich. Sie geht in die kleine Küche und schreit sehr laut. In der gemütlichen Küche ist ein dicker Koch. Der runde Koch hat eine große Nase. Der böße Koch sagt: "Wieviel Euros kostet ein Mercedes?" Die gute Frau Müller fällt in Ohnmacht.

Mrs. Müller.

On Wednesday the beautiful Mrs. Müller goes to the little café in Rosenheim. The cute Mrs. Müller orders a hot coffee. The friendly waitress brings coffee to the pretty Mrs. Müller. But the coffee is cold. Now the lovely Mrs. Müller screams: "The coffee is horrible!" The slow waitress comes to the wild Mrs.

Müller and says: "The coffee is not cold." Mrs. Müller is angry. She goes into the little kitchen and screams very loud. In the cozy kitchen is a fat cook. The round cook has a huge nose. The evil cook says: "How many euros costs a Mercedes?" The good Mrs. Müller faints.

Once the students have written down the dictation into their workbooks, a final reading of the whole text is being done. Then copies of the text are handed out to the students, and the students are asked to check their spelling. An evaluation scale is given on the blackboard, typically allowing for one mistake per line as "sehr gut" (very good), 2 mistakes per line as "gut" (good), 3 mistakes per line as "auch gut" (still good), four mistakes or more as "nicht so gut" (not that good).

Frau Müller (mit etwas Englisch).
Am Mittwoch geht die schöne Frau Müller zu dem kleinen Café in Rosenheim. Die nette Frau Müller sagt: "Hot coffee, please. And be quick about it!" Die freundliche Bedienung bringt der hübschen Frau Müller Kaffee, und sagt: "Here is your cold coffee, stupid cow!" Da schreit die liebe Frau Müller: "The coffee is awful!" Frau Müller ist ärgerlich. Sie geht in die kleine Küche und schreit: "I am having a bad day!" In der gemütlichen Küche ist ein dicker Koch. Der runde Koch hat eine große Nase. Der böße Koch sagt: "Do you want some candied pig's innards?" Die gute Frau Müller fällt in Ohnmacht.

Frau Müller (with bits of English).
On Wednesday the beautiful Mrs. Müller goes to the little café in Rosenheim. The nice Mrs. Müller says: "Hot coffee, please. And be quick about it!" The

friendly waitress brings the pretty Mrs. Müller coffee, and says: "Here is your cold coffee, stupid cow!" Now the lovely Mrs. Müller screams: "The coffee is awful!" Mrs. Müller is angry. She goes into the little kitchen and screams: "I am having a bad day!" In the cozy kitchen is a fat cook. The round cook has a huge nose. The evil cook says: "Do you want some candied pig's innards?" The good Mrs. Müller faints.

Once the students have checked and corrected their spelling, they are asked to translate the dictation into English – this might also constitute their homework assignment.

Ein Diktat in depressiver Stimmung.

Mittags geht Heribert zu dem grauen Café hinter dem Bürohaus. Das Café hat schwarze Wände, und braune Tische mit grauen Stühlen. Heribert bestellt schwarzen Kaffee, Schokoladentorte, und zwei graue Heringe. Das Essen kommt auf schwarzen Tellern. Die Bedienung trägt schwarze Hosen, braune Handschuhe und schwarzes Make-up.

A dictation in depressive mood.

At noon Heribert goes to the gray café behind the office building. The café has black walls, and brown tables with gray chairs. Heribert orders black coffee, chocolate pie, and two gray herrings. The food arrives on black plates. The waitress wears black pants, brown gloves and black make-up.

A variation is to give the students the task to complete sentences given in a dictation or to insert sentences or replies. I typically give the students a few minutes to create their inserts, then ask some of them to share their creations, which brings about a more participatory atmosphere.

Frau Müller (Variation).

Am Mittwoch geht die schöne Frau Müller zu dem kleinen Café in Rosenheim. Die nette Frau Müller bestellt einen heißen Kaffee und .... Die freundliche Bedienung bringt der hübschen Frau Müller Kaffee. Aber der Kaffee ist kalt. Da schreit die liebe Frau Müller: "Der Kaffee ist fürchterlich!" Die langsame Bedienung kommt zu der wilden Frau Müller und sagt: "...................." Frau Müller ist ärgerlich. Sie geht in die kleine Küche und schreit sehr laut. In der gemütlichen Küche ist ein dicker Koch. Der runde Koch hat eine große Nase. Der böße Koch sagt: "................................" Die gute Frau Müller fällt in Ohnmacht.

Mrs. Müller (variation).

On Wednesday the beautiful Mrs. Müller goes to the little café in Rosenheim. The cute Mrs. Müller orders a hot coffee and .... The friendly waitress brings coffee to the pretty Mrs. Müller. But the coffee is cold. Now the lovely Mrs. Müller screams: "The coffee is horrible!" The slow waitress comes to the wild Mrs. Müller and says: "................." Mrs. Müller is angry. She goes into the little kitchen and screams very loud. In the cozy kitchen is a fat cook. The round cook has a huge nose. The evil cook says: "..................?" The good Mrs. Müller faints.

Frau Unsinn.

Am Montag geht die schöne Frau Unsinn zu dem kleinen Café in Stuttgart. Die blöde Frau Unsinn bestellt zwei Wiener Schnitzel, einen heißen Kaffee, und eine Erdbeertorte mit Schlagsahne. Die große Bedienung bringt der müden Frau Unsinn alles. Aber der Kaffee ist zu dünn, das Schnitzel ist kalt, und die Torte ist schrecklich. Die Schlagsahne ist grün und stinkt. Frau Unsinn wartet bis die Bedienung zurück kommt. Dann spuckt Frau Unsinn in den Kaffee. Sie wirft das Wiener Schnitzel an die Wand, und schreit: "Bezahlen, bitte!"

Mrs. Nonsense.

On Monday the beautiful Mrs. Nonsense goes to the little cafe in Stuttgart. The stupid Mrs. Nonsense orders two veal cutlets Viennese, a hot coffee, and a strawberry torte with whipping cream. The tall waitress brings the tired Mrs. Nonsense everything. But the coffee is too thin, the cutlet is cold, and the torte is horrible. The whipping cream is green and stinks. Mrs. Nonsense waits until the waitress comes back. Then Mrs. Nonsense spits into the coffee. She throws the veal cutlet Viennese against the wall, and screams: "Check, please!"

Einfach und kurz.

Fünfzehn Mädchen wohnen in einer Stadt in Deutschland. Warum regnet es jeden Tag? Helmut ißt einen Hamburger in Hamburg. Der Zug fährt von Berlin nach Moskau. Der Frosch fällt in das Wasser und ist tot. Der Fisch liegt auf dem Teller und lacht.

Simple and short.

Fifteen girls live in a city in Germany. Why does it rain every day? Helmut eats a hamburger in Hamburg. The train travels from Berlin to Moscow. The frog falls into the water and is dead. The fish lies on the plate and laughs.

Der Tag der Bäume.

Heute ist Mittwoch, der 9. Januar. Am Donnerstag geht Herr Meier in den Wald. Herr Meier hat einen Spaten. Er will einen Baum pflanzen. Warum? Ja, Herr Meier hat ein schlechtes Gewissen. Am Montag hat Herr Meier einen Baum gefällt. Die Polizei sagte zu Herrn Meier: "Du mußt einen Baum pflanzen, oder du gehst für 50 Jahre in das Gefängnis."

Arbor Day.

Today is Wednesday January 9th. On Thursday Mr. Meier goes into the forest. Mr. Meier has a spade. He wants to plant a tree. Why? Well, Mr. Meier has a bad conscience. On Monday Mr. Meier cut down a tree. The police told Mr. Meier: "You need to plant a tree, or you will go to prison for 50 years."

Another variation is to include questions in the dictation, which the students have to answer, or to ask them to identify the *4 Fälle, the 4 cases* in a sentence: *Nominativ, Genetiv, Dativ, Akkusativ*

Otto.

Otto von Bismark fährt mit der U-Bahn nach Berlin. Warum? In der Turmstraße ist ein kleines, dunkles Büro. Ich liebe den heißen Kaffee mit dem weichem Kartoffelbrei und dem kaltem Hering. (Fälle). Warum ist Berlin die Hauptstadt von Deutschland? Wieviel Menschen leben in Berlin? Warum leben die Menschen in Berlin?

Otto. Otto von Bismark travels with the subway to Berlin. Why? In the Tower Street there is a small, dark office. I love the hot coffee with the soft mashed potatoes and the cold herring. (Cases). Why is Berlin the capitol of Germany? How many people live in Berlin? Why do people live in Berlin?

Der gelbe Marsmensch.

Der gelbe Marsmensch fliegt mit dem mickrigen UFO über den grünen Wald trotz des Nieselregens. (Fälle). Warum hat der Marsmensch so große Ohren und so lange Haare? Antwort: .... Ich bin außerhalb der Schule, und innerhalb der Stadt, und oberhalb der Erde, und unterhalb des Himmels, und inmitten der Häuser, und gegenüber dem Freund. Wo bin ich? Antwort: .... Frau Schocker rennt mit dem riesigen Hund gegen das rote Haus während der Mittagspause. (Fälle). Warum? Antwort: ....

The yellow Martian.

The yellow Martian flies with the cheap UFO over the green forest in spite of the drizzling rain. (Cases). Why has the Martian such huge ears and such long hair? Answer: .... I am outside the school, and within the city, and above the earth, and below the sky, and in the middle of the houses, and opposite the friend. Where am I? Answer: .... Mrs. Shocker races with the gigantic dog against the red house during lunch break. (Cases). Why? Answer: ....

Der grüne Marsmensch.

Der grüne Marsmensch fliegt mit dem mickrigen UFO über den gelben Wald trotz des Nieselregens.

(Fälle). Warum hat der Marsmensch so große Ohren und so lange Haare? Antwort: .... Heribert fährt mit dem Moped der Susi durch die Stadt. (Fälle). Susi hat einen roten Helm auf den roten Haaren. Wo bin ich? Antwort: .... Frau Schocker rennt mit dem riesigen Hund gegen das rote Haus des Herrn Müller. (Fälle). Warum? Antwort: .... Susi geht zu dem Supermarkt und kauft ein Stück Hammelfleisch mit einem Knochen darin. Warum? Antwort: ....

The green Martian.

The green Martian flies with the cheap UFO over the yellow forest in spite of the drizzling rain. (Cases). Why has the Martian such huge ears and such long hair? Answer: .... Heribert rides the moped belonging to Susi through the city. (Cases). Susi has a red helmet on the red hair. Where am I? Answer: .... Mrs. Shocker races with the gigantic dog against the red house belonging to Mr. Müller. (Cases).Why? Answer: .... Susi goes to the supermarket and buys a piece of mutton with a bone in it. Why? Answer: ....

Still another option is to paint a picture with words via the dictation, and then have the students first translate the dictation, and then draw or paint the scene described.

Beim Teetrinken.
Herr Schröder und Herr Stoiber trinken Tee. Da sagt Herr Stoiber: "Gerhard, der Tee schmeckt komisch!" Herr Schröder sagt: "Mir schmeckt der Tee ganz gut." Herr Stoiber fragt: "Was für ein Tee ist das?" Herr Schröder antwortet: "Das ist grüner Tee. Hahaha!"

At tea.
Mr. Schröder and Mr. Stoiber drink tea. Then says Mr. Stoiber: "Gerhard, the tea tastes funny!" Mr. Schröder says: "I like the taste of the tea." Mr. Stoiber asks: "What kind of tea is this?" Mr. Schröder answers: „This is green tea. Hahaha!"

Der Salat und der Tiger.

Der Salat ist grün. Die Milch ist kalt. Die Tomate ist rot. Der Tiger ist alt und elegant. Der Tiger ißt die Suppe. Die Suppe ist warm. Der Tiger ißt die Tomate nicht. Der Tiger hat eine Trompete. Das Zebra geht zu der Universität in Chicago. Die Tomate haßt das Sandwich. Der Tourist sitzt auf dem Sofa in der Garage. Der Präsident ist blond und hat Hunger. Der Winter ist intelligent. Das Radio ist laut. Der Pullover ist gelb und grün. Die Vase ist kaputt. Weißt Du wieviel Sternlein stehen an dem blauen Himmelszelt? Fünfundsechzig?

The salad and the tiger.

The salad is green. The milk is cold. The tomato is red. The tiger is old and elegant. The tiger eats the soup. The soup is warm. The tiger doesn't eat the tomato. The tiger has a trumpet. The zebra goes to the university in Chicago. The tomato hates the sandwich. The tourist sits on the sofa in the garage. The president is blond and is hungry. The winter is intelligent. The radio is loud. The pullover is yellow and green. The vase is broken. Do you know how many stars there are in the sky? Sixty five?

The following dictation consists of 10 questions. The students are expected to answer the questions in German. Usually the students are asked to share some of their answers, which create a new level of involvement and a great atmosphere of participation.

1. *Wo bin ich?*
2. *Wo bitte ist Kansas City?*
3. *Welche Farbe hat die U-Bahn?*
4. *Welche Farbe hat der Schnee?*
5. *Kann ich mit der Kreditkarte Kanu fahren?*
6. *Wieviel kostet eine halbe Banane?*
7. *Wo ist ein Kaufhaus namens Wal-Mart?*
8. *Wo ist ein Supermarkt?*
9. *Wo ist eine schlechte Bäckerei?*
10. *Wo ist mein Papa?*

1. *Where am I?*
2. *Where please is Kansas City?*
3. *What color is the subway?*
4. *What color is the snow?*
5. *Can I use the credit card to go canoeing?*
6. *How much is half a banana?*
7. *Where is the store called Wal-Mart?*
8. *Where is a supermarket?*
9. *Where is a bad bakery?*
10. *Where is my dad?*

The next dictation has several tasks for the students. First the students are asked to identify all nouns by underlining them in one color, next all verbs are underlined in another color, and finally appropriate adjectives are inserted. This can also be given as a homework assignment.

Der Bauer.

Franz Beckenbauer war ein .... Bauer. Er lebte mit seiner .... Frau und mit 33 .... Schweinen und 36 .... Kühen in einem kleinen .... Dorf. In dem .... Dorf gab es auch ein .... Wirtshaus und eine .... Kirche. Am Sonntag ging Herr Beckenbauer und Frau Beckenbauer in die .... Kirche. Dann ging Frau Beckenbauer nach .... Hause und Herr Beckenbauer ging in das .... Wirtshaus. Das .... Wirtshaus hieß "Zum Wilden Schwein"; dort gab es .... Bier und .... Limonade, ... Wurst und .... Brot. Herr Beckenbauer liebte .... Bier, ... Wurst und .... Brot. Am Abend ging Herr Beckenbauer nach Hause zu seinem .... Bauernhof. Er mußte 25 .... Kühe melken und 33 .... Schweine füttern. Was für ein schönes Leben!

The farmer.

Franz Beckenbauer was a .... farmer. He lived with his .... wife and with 33 .... pigs and 36 .... cows in a little .... village. In the .... village there was also a .... tavern and a .... church. On Sunday Mr. and Mrs. Beckenbauer went to the .... church. Then Mrs. Beckenbauer went .... home and Mr. Beckenbauer went to the ....

tavern. The .... tavern was called "The Wild Pig"; there they had .... beer and .... lemonade, ... sausage and .... bread. Mr. Beckenbauer loved .... beer, ... sausage and .... bread. In the evening Mr. Beckenbauer went home to his .... farmstead. He had to milk 25 .... cows and to feed 33 .... pigs. What a beautiful life!

Another variation of this theme is to ask the students to again identify the nouns, verbs, and adjectives, and then interchange the verbs and adjectives to create a new and different story.

Der Bauer II.

Heribert ist ein kleiner Bauer. Er lebt mit seiner lieben Frau und mit 33 fetten Schweinen und 36 winzigen Kühen in einem kleinen Dorf. In dem schönen Dorf gibt es auch ein Wirtshaus und eine Kirche. Am Sonntag geht Heribert in die Kirche. Dann geht Heribert in das komische Wirtshaus. Das Wirtshaus heißt "Zum Wilden Schwein". Dort gibt es Bier und Limonade, Wurst und Brot. Heribert liebt Bier, Wurst und Brot. Am Abend geht Heribert nach Hause zu seinem Bauernhof. Er muß 25 Kühe melken und 33 Schweine füttern. Was für ein schönes Leben!

The Farmer II.

Heribert is a small farmer. He lives with his lovely wife and with 33 fat pigs and 36 tiny cows in a little village. In the beautiful village there is also a tavern and a church. On Sunday Heribert goes to the church. Then Heribert goes to the comical tavern. The tavern is called "The Wild Pig". There you get beer and lemonade, sausage and bread. Heribert loves beer, sausage and bread. In the evening Heribert goes home to his farmstead. He has to milk 25 cows and to feed 33 pigs. What a beautiful life!

The next dictation is one that the students were asked to create by each contributing a sentence or two, bringing their experiences and interests into the story.

Bauerngeschichten.

Nate: Die Kuh und die Kälber gehen zu dem Weideland. Sie essen zwei Kartoffeln, ein Insekt, und viele Gräser. Die Gans fliegt über dem Kopf. Die Kuh sagt: "Da geht die Gans. Sie ist nicht eine fette Kuh." Das Kalb sagt: "Ja, das stimmt, aber die Gans fliegt schnell."

Ben: Ich habe fünf Gänse. Du wohnst in einem Bauernhaus. Da ißt du viele Pflanzen. Und vielleicht eine kleine Maus.

Ita: Der Morgen auf dem Bauernhof ist neu. Der Hahn schläft jetzt während der Hund um das Haus schleicht. Das Pferd ißt Gras auf dem Feld und die Sonne geht langsam auf.

Ben: Ich gehe zu dem Bauerhof und züchte einen rohen, fetten, natürlichen Fisch.

Anton: Die Kühe welche wir essen, sie essen das Heu, welches ißt das CO_2, welches wir mit unseren Autos machen.

Theo: Ich gehe zu meinem Bauer, weil ich mein Getreide ernten will. Denn ich will von meinem Getreide Mehl machen. Denn ich will mit meinem Mehl zu dem Bauernmarkt gehen.

Georgia: Heute erlebt ein Schwein einen kalten Morgen ausserhalb und die Katze erlebt einen warmen Morgen innerhalb des Hauses. Die Katze hat Milch zum Frühstück und das Schwein hat das Gras.

Farmers' stories.

Nate: The cow and the calves go to the pasture. They eat two potatoes, one insect, and lots of grass. The goose flies above the head. The cow says: "There goes the goose. She is not a fat cow." The calf says: "Yes, that is true, but the goose flies fast."

Ben: I have five geese. You live in a farmhouse. There you eat lots of plants. And perhaps a little mouse.

Ita: The morning at the farmstead is new. The rooster sleeps now, while the dog creeps past the house. The horse eats grass in the field and the sun slowly rises.

Ben: I go to the farmstead and raise a raw, fat, natural fish.

Anton: The cows which we eat, they eat the hay, which eats the CO_2, which we produce with our cars.

Theo: I go to my farmer, because I want to harvest my grain. Because I want to make flour out of my grain. Because I want to go with my flour to the farmers' market.

Georgia: Today a pig experiences a cold morning outside and a cat experiences a warm morning inside the house. The cat has milk for breakfast and the pig has grass.

It is a good idea to introduce a tragicomic hero or heroine, and have him (or her) appear again and again in the stories and exercises. *Heribert* is such a hero; based on one of my childhood friends, he became over time our hero and friend in class ...

Heribert und der Fisch.

Heribert hat einen Fisch. Der Fisch ist tot und stinkt. Heribert hat ein Haus. Das Haus ist rot und schief. Heribert geht snowborden. Er hat ein hübsches blaues Snowbord. Heribert ist glücklich!

Heribert and the fish.

Heribert has a fish. The fish is dead and stinks. Heribert has a house. The house is red and crooked. Heribert goes snowboarding. He has a pretty blue snowboard. Heribert is happy!

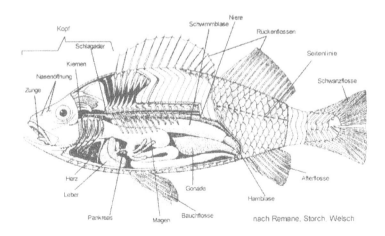

nach Remane, Storch, Welsch

A dictation can contain instructions leading to an activity. *Heriberts Abenteuer Nummer 18* includes a cookies recipe that the students can be asked to distill from the dictation, bring in the ingredients to a following session, and prepare a batch of fine tasking cookies to share with the French class students ...

Heriberts Abenteuer Nummer 18.

Susi schreit: "Heribert, backe sofort ein paar Kekse für mich!" Heribert fährt mit seinem Moped zum Supermarkt und kauft 500 g Mehl, 450 g Zucker, 1 Päckchen Backpulver, 1 Päckchen Vanillezucker, 12 Eier, und 223 g süße Sahne. Er denkt: "Süße Sahne für die süße Susi." Heribert rast zurück nach Hause. Er mixt die Zutaten und formt einen festen Teig. Dann rollt er den Teig dünn aus und sticht kleine runde Kreise aus. Er bäckt die Kekse in seinem Backofen bei 180 Grad Celcius für 15 Minuten. Susi kocht Kaffee. Susi und Heribert trinken schwarzen Kaffee und essen 25 Kekse. Das schmeckt gut!

Heribert's adventure number 18.

Susi screams: "Heribert, bake at once some cookies for me!" Heribert rides his moped to the supermarket and buys 500 gram flour, 450 gram sugar, 1 box of baking powder, 1 box of vanilla sugar, 12 eggs, and 223 gram sweet (heavy) cream. He thinks: "Sweet cream for the sweet Susi." Heribert races back home. He mixes the ingredients and makes a stiff dough. Then he rolls out the dough thinly and cuts little round circles. He bakes the cookies in his baking oven at 180 degrees Celsius for 15 minutes. Susi makes coffee. Susi and Heribert drink black coffee and eat 25 cookies. That tastes good!

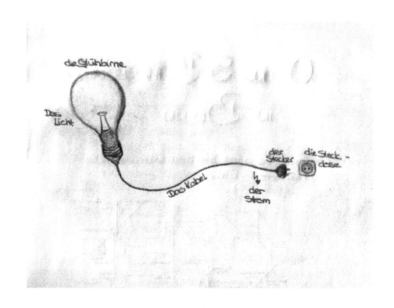

Die Abenteuer des Heribert oder Heriberts Abenteuer --- Teil Fünfzehn.

Heribert hat ein Haus welches schön, groß, blau, und nett ist. Heribert hat das Haus selber gebaut. Er geht jeden Tag zum Do-It-Yourself-Center und kauft Glühbirnen, Kabel, Steckdosen, Stecker, und einen Schraubenzieher. Heribert installiert die Steckdose an der Wand. Er befestigt die Glühbirne an der Decke und legt das Kabel von der Glühbirne bis zu der Steckdose. Dann steckt Heribert den Stecker in die Steckdose und plötzlich geht das Licht an. Heribert telefoniert sofort die Susi und sagt: "Susi, komme sofort zu meinem Haus. Ich habe Licht!" Es ist vierzehn Uhr. Susi fährt mit dem Moped zu Heriberts Haus. Sie schaut durch das Fenster in das Haus. Das Licht ist an und Heribert steckt gerade den Schraubenzieher in die Steckdose. Heriberts Haar steht senkrecht und sein Mund ist offen. Susi schreit: "Halt!" Heribert läßt den Schraubenzieher fallen und rennt zu dem Fenster. Das war knapp!

The adventures of Heribert or Heribert's adventures --- part fifteen.

Heribert has a house which is beautiful, big, blue, and nice. Heribert built the house himself. He goes every day to the Do-It-Yourself-Center and buys light bulbs, wire, outlets, plugs, and a screw driver. Heribert installs the outlet at the wall. He fastens the light bulb at the ceiling and lays the wire from the light bulb to the outlet. Then Heribert puts the plug into the outlet and suddenly the light goes on. Heribert phones Susi at once and says: "Susi, come over at once to my house. I have light!" It is 2 PM. Susi rides the moped to Heribert's house. She looks through the window into the house. The light is on and Heribert is just now putting the screw driver into the outlet. Heribert's hair sticks up straight and his mouth is open. Susi screams: "Stop!" Heribert drops the screw driver and races to the window. That was close!

Heribert reist nach Westby.

Am Samstag geht Heribert zu Susi nach Westby. Heribert nimmt die U-Bahn von Viroqua nach Westby-Mitte. Dann fährt Heribert mit dem Bus nach Westby-Süd. Susi wohnt in der Schnorkelsonstraße fünfundsiebzig. Susi liebt Hammelfleisch. Susi kocht Hammelfleischbraten mit Tomaten, Knoblauch und Gurken für den lieben Heribert. Heribert lacht und sagt: "Vielen Dank. Leider bin ich ein Vegetarier und ich hasse Hammelfleisch."

Heribert travels to Westby.

On Saturday Heribert goes to Susi in Westby. Heribert takes the subway from Viroqua to Westby-Midtown. Then Heribert takes the bus to South Westby. Susi lives in the Schnorkelson Street seventy five. Susi loves mutton. Susi cooks mutton roast with tomatoes, garlic and cucumbers for the lovely Heribert. Heribert laughs and says: "Thank you very much. Pity I am a vegetarian and I hate mutton."

Heribert im Schneesturm.

Heribert hat ein Auto. Am Dienstag fährt Heribert nach Rosenheim. Das Auto ist ein Mercedes A120. Heribert fährt auf der Autobahn mit 120 km/h. Warum? .... Das Wetter ist schlecht. Der Wind pfeift aus Südost. Ein Orkan bläst aus Südwest. Plötzlich kommt ein Schneesturm. Heribert schaltet den Scheibenwischer an. Was sagt Heribert? .... Die Temperatur ist -12 C. Heribert nimmt sein Handy und telephoniert seine Großmutter. Heribert sagt: "Oma, es schneit ganz schrecklich. Ich habe Angst." Was sagt Oma? ....

Heribert in the snowstorm.

Heribert has a car. On Tuesday Heribert drives to Rosenheim. The car is a Mercedes A120. Heribert drives on the interstate at 120 km/h. Why? .... The weather is bad. The wind whistles from Southwest. Suddely a snowstorm arrives. Heribert turns on the windshield wipers. What does

Heribert say? ……………….. The temperature is 112 C. Heribert takes his mobile phone and phones his grandma. Heribert says: "Grandma, it snows really terribly. I am afraid." What does Grandma say? ………………….

Heribert reist nach München.

Am Samstag geht Heribert zu Susi nach München. Heribert nimmt die S-Bahn von Türkenfeld nach Hauptbahnhof. Dann fährt er mit der U-Bahn nach Schwabing. Susi wohnt in der Leopoldstraße 356 1/2 B. Susi ist Vegetarierin. Sie kocht Sojaburger und Grünkern für den lieben Heribert. Heribert lacht und trinkt eine Limonade.

Heribert travels to Munich.

On Saturday Heribert goes to Susi in Munich. Heribert takes the train from Türkenfeld to Main Train Station. Then he travels with the subway to Schwabing. Susi lives at Leopold Street 356 ½ B. Susi is a vegatarian. She cooks soy burgers and Grünkorn (a wheat variety) for the lovely Heribert. Heribert laughs and drinks a lemonade.

37

Heribert ißt einen Hamburger.

Heute ist Donnerstag, der 30. Mai 2... Die Sonne scheint durch die Wolkendecke, und der Schneesturm hat viel Feuchtigkeit. Das ist geschmacklos. Warum regnet es jeden Tag? Der Regenbogen lebt in Westby. Das ist köstlich. Heribert ißt einen Hamburger in Hamburg. Heribert ist kein Sojaburger. Heribert heißt Heribert. Der Sojaburger heißt nicht Heribert. Wie heißt der Sojaburger? Heribert und Susi gehen Eis essen. Heribert liebt Schokolade, Susi haßt Schokolade. Susi sagt: "Schokoladeneis ist braun, und schmeckt verfault. Ich esse lieber Vanilleeis." Susi und Heribert gehen einkaufen. Sie kaufen tote Fische, grüne Hosen, und Make-up. Heribert sagt: "Susi, du bist doof. Das Make-up ist schwarz und rot. Ich mag das nicht."

Heribert eats a hamburger.

Today is Thursday May 30, 2... The sun shines through the cloud cover, and the snowstorm brings lots of moisture. That is tasteless. Why does it rain every day? The rainbow lives in Westby. That is tasty. Heribert eats a hamburger in Hamburg. Heribert is not a soy burger. Heribert is called Heribert. The soy burger is not called Heribert. What is the soy burger called. Heribert and Susi go to eat icecream. Heribert loves chocolade, Susi hates chocolate. Susi says: "Chocolate icecream is brown, and tastes rotten. I prefer to eat vanilla icecream." Susi and Heribert go shopping. They buy dead fish, green pants, and make-up. Heribert says: "Susi, you are stupid. The make-up is black and red. I don't like it."

Giving and asking for directions is an important skill, and can be incorporated into dictations as well. The following dictation includes such an exercise and works with a map of the Munich railroad/subway system. This can easily be accommodated to different situations and available maps.

Heribert in München.

Heribert fliegt nach München via New York und Helsinki. Heribert muß durch die Paßkontrolle. Was sagt der Polizist zu Heribert? .... Am Flughafen München trinkt Heribert eine Fanta. Dann geht er zu der S-Bahn. Heribert muß nach Höllriegelskreuth fahren. (Wegbeschreibung). Heribert besucht Susi in Höllriegelskreuth. Susi wohnt in einem Apartment in der Donnervogelstraße 368. (Wegbeschreibung). Sie hat zwei Zimmer und eine Küche, zwei Katzen und einen Vogel. Der Vogel fliegt nach Poing. Susi und Heribert fahren sofort nach Poing. (Wegbeschreibung). Susi und Heribert fangen ihren Vogel mit einem Netz. Dann gehen sie Onkel Helmuth besuchen. Onkel Helmuth wohnt *nahe der Haltestelle Brudermühlstraße. (Wegbeschreibung).*

Heribert in Munich.

Heribert flies to Munich via New York and Helsinki. Heribert has to go through the passport controls. What does the policeman say to Heribert? ……………….. At the Munich airport Heribert drinks a Fanta. Then he goes to the train. Heribert has to go to Höllriegelskreuth. (Directions). Heribert visits Susi in Höllriegelskreuth. Susi lives in an apartment in the Thunderbird Street 368. (Directions). She has two rooms and a kitchen, two cats and one bird. The bird flies to Poing. Susi and Heribert travel at once to Poing. (Directions). Susi and Heribert catch their bird with a net. Then they go visit uncle Helmuth. Uncle Helmuth lives near the stop Brudermühlstraße. (Directions).

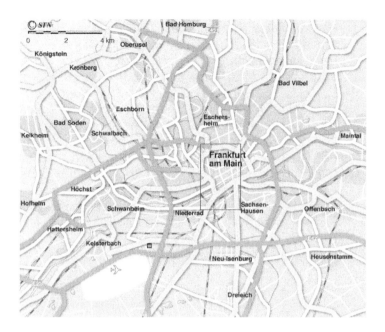

Heribert verirrt sich.

Heribert fliegt von Moskau nach Frankfurt. Er landet am Flughafen und geht zu McDonald's, wo er Pommes mit Ketchup ißt. Dann mietet Heribert ein Mietauto bei Budget. Was für ein Auto bekommt er? Antwort: .... Heribert fährt nach rechts auf die Autobahn A3 bis Neu-Isenburg. Dann nimmt er die B3 nach Süden. Er fährt circa 5 km. Wo ist er jetzt? Antwort: .... Heribert verfährt sich. Das ist schade. Plötzlich ist Heribert in Bad Vilbel. Wie kam Heribert nach Bad Vilbel? Antwort: .... Heribert's Handy klingelt. Es ist Susi! Sie sagt: "Heribert, mein Süßer, ich bin in Frankfurt am Flughafen. Komme schnell!" (Beschreibe den Weg von Bad Vilbel zum Flughafen und schätze wie lange es dauert).

Heribert gets lost.

Heribert flies from Moscow to Frankfurt. He lands at the airport and goes to McDonalds, where he eats fries with ketchup. Then Heribert rents a rental car at Budget. What kind of car does he get? Answer: .... Heribert drives to the right onto the Interstate A3 to Neu-Isenberg. Then he takes the B3 towards the South. He drives for approximately 5 km. Where is he now? Answer: .... Heribert gets lost. What a pity. Suddenly Heribert is in Bad Vilbel. How did Heribert get to Bad Vilbel? Answer: .... Heribert's mobile phone rings. It is Susi! She says: "Heribert, my sweetheart, I am in Frankfurt at the airport. Come quickly!" (Describe the way from Bad Vilbel to the airport and give an estimate of how long it will take.)

Here we learn about parts of the human body ...

Heriberts Abenteuer XXII.

Heribert ist ein junger Mann. Er hat schwarze Haare und zwei Ohren. Er hat eine Nase im Gesicht. Sein Mund ist manchmal offen. Er hat blaue Augen und fünf Finger an der rechten Hand. Wo ist sein Herz? Antwort: .... Heribert's Freundin ist Susi. Susi hat sieben Ohrringe, eine kurze Nase, und lange, rote Haare. Susi und Heribert gehen Hand in Hand zu dem .... Heribert kauft .... und Susi sagt: .... Susi fällt wegen dem Glatteis auf den Hintern. Das tut weh! Heribert trägt Susi zu seinem Auto. Susi's Arm hängt an Heribert's Hals. Dann ....

Heribert's adventure XXII.

Heribert is a young man. He has black hair and two ears. He has a nose in his face. His mouth sometimes hangs open. He has blue eyes and five fingers on his right hand. Where is his heart? Answer: ……………….. Heribert's friend is Susi. Susi has seven earrings, a short nose, and long, red hair. Susi and Heribert hold hands while going to ……………….. Heribert buys ……………….. and Susi says ……………….. Susi falls because of the black ice on her behind. That hurts! Heribert carries Susi to his car. Susi's arm is slung around Heribert's neck. Then ………………..

Katarina's Reise #1. (von Ita Rehbach)

Katarina macht eine Reise. Sie geht zu ihrer Freundin. Die Freundin heisst Amelie. Katarina spaziert zum Hauptbahnhof. Unterwegs geht sie in eine Bäckerei und kauft zwei Stück Apfelkuchen. Dann geht sie auf die Strasse und sie geht nach links statt nach rechts. Sie hat sich verlaufen. Plötzlich sieht sie einen alten Mann. Sie sagt zu dem alten Mann, "Entschuldigung, wo ist der Hauptbahnhof?" Der alte Mann antwortet, "Ich weiss nicht, frage doch meinen Freund Piet." Aber wo ist Piet? Piet ist ein Hobo, und lebt in einer grossen Schachtel. Katarina fragt Piet, "Entschuldigung, wo ist der Hauptbahnhof?" Und Piet antwortet, "Nehmen Sie die Hauptstrasse nach Süden bis zur Ahornstrasse, dann links in die Ahornstrasse bis zu der Bibliothek und dann rechts, und geradeaus für eine Weile immer der Nase nach bis zu dem Hauptbahnhof." Dann fährt sie mit dem Zug bis nach Rosenplatz und besucht Amelie. Das Ende.

Katarina's journey #1. (by Ita Rehbach)

Katarina goes on a journey. She visits her friend. The friend is called Amelie. Katarina strolls to the Main Train Station. On the way she stops at a bakery and buys two pieces of apple pie. Then she goes onto the street and turns left instead of right. She is lost. Suddenly she sees an old man. She says to the old man, "Excuse me, where is the Main Train Station?" The old man replies, "I don't know, ask my friend Piet." But where is Piet? Piet is a hobo, and lives in a huge box. Katarina asks Piet, "Excuse me, where is the Main Train Station?" And Piet answers, „Take the Main Street towards South until Maple Street, then left on Maple Street up to the library and then right, and straight ahead for a while – follow your nose – all the way to the Main Train Station." Then she takes the train to Rosenplatz and visits Amelie. The end.

Am Mittwoch.

Am Mittwoch geht die häßliche Frau Müller zu dem schrecklichen Café in Rosenheim. Sie sagt: "Cold coffee, please. And be quick about it!" Die fürchterliche Bedienung bringt der mickrigen Frau Müller den Kaffee, und sagt: "Here is your rotten coffee, with pieces of mutton in it!" Da schreit die dumme Frau Müller: "Thank you very much. I love it!"

On Wednesday.

On Wednesday the ugly Mrs. Müller goes to the terrible café in Rosenheim. She says: "Kalter Kaffee, bitte. Und schnell!" The horrible waitress brings coffee to the tiny Mrs. Müller, and says: "Hier ist Ihr verfaulter Kaffee, mit Hammelfleischstücken darin!" Now screams the stupid Mrs. Müller: "Vielen Dank. Ich liebe es!"

Some of my favorite dictations include murder mysteries. Certain hints and clues are part of the story, and, by carefully listening, a student will be able to identify the culprit. Following you will find a few examples.

Ein Mord.

Heribert und Susi gehen zu einer Party. Dort sehen sie Franz-Heinrich, Herr Frosty Schneemann, Frau Schnorkelson aus Westby, Gerhard Schröder, Angela Merkel und Alex. Heribert drinkt Fanta und Susi hat ein Spezi. Franz-Heinrich singt ein Lied: "La la la la und lala!" Gerhard Schröder und Frau Schnorkelson machen Musik. Sie sind Punkrocker. Angela Merkel und Alex reden über die guten alten Zeiten und Herr Frosty Schneemann ißt Tofuchips. Plötzlich geht das Licht aus. Stille. Ein Schrei: "AAAAAHHHHHHH!!!!!!!" Dann Stille. Das Licht geht wieder an. Franz-Heinrich liegt tot auf dem Boden in einer Blutlache. Mord! Der Herr Kommissar Müller kommt sofort mit seinem BMW 740 tii. Kommissar Müller untersucht den Fall. Heribert hat eine Pistole. Susi hat ein Feuerzeug. Herr Frosty Schneemann hat ein großes Messer. Frau Schnorkelson hat eine Motorsäge. Gerhard Schröder hat eine Bombe. Angela Merkel hat ein Maschinengewehr und Alex hat Durchfall. Der Kommissar sagt sofort: "Der Mörder ist ....!" (Warum?)

Murder.

Heribert and Susi go to a party. There they see Franz-Heinrich, Mr. Frosty Snowman, Mrs. Schnorkelson from Westby, Gerhard Schröder, Angela Merkel and Alex. Heribert drinks Fanta and Susi has a Spezi (cola/lemonade mix). Franz-Heinrich sings a song: "La la la la and lala!" Gerhard Schröder and Mrs. Schnorkelson make music. They are punk rockers. Angela Merkel and Alex converse *about the good old days and Mr. Frosty Snowman eats tofu chips. Suddenly the lights go out. Stillness. A scream: "AAAAAHHHHHHH!!!!!!" Then stillness. The light comes on again. Franz-Heinrich lies dead on the floor in a puddle of blood. Murder! Inspector Müller arrives at once in his BMW 740 tii. Inspector Müller investigates the case. Heribert has a pistol. Susi has a lighter. Mr. Frosty Snowman has a large knife. Mrs. Schnorkelson has a chain saw. Gerhard Schröder has a bomb. Angela Merkel has a machine gun and Alex has diarrhea. The inspector says at once: "The murderer is ………………..!" (Why?)*

Herr Frosty Schneemann is the culprit, as he is the only one with a noiseless weapon.

Ein Mord 2.

Susi und Heribert haben einen Plan. Sie wollen etwas essen und danach in das Kino gehen. Susi und Heribert fahren mit Heribert's Moped nach Westby zu Borgen's Café. Sie gehen in das Café und setzen sich an einen Tisch und bestellen zwei Fanta und Pommes Frites mit Majonäse und zwei Würste mit Senf. In dem Café sind auch Franz-Heinrich, Herr Frosty Schneemann, Frau Schnorkelson, Gerhard Schröder, Angela Merkel und Alex. Franz-Heinrich bestellt Tofuchips. Herr Frosty Schneemann ist der Koch. Er kommt aus der Küche und singt ein Lied: "La la la dum dum da da und lala!" Gerhard Schröder und Frau Schnorkelson singen ein Jodelduett. Frau Schnorkelson ist die Bedienung. Angela Merkel und Alex reden (wie immer) über die guten alten Zeiten. Frau Schorkelson bringt erst Franz-Heinrich, dann Susi und Heribert das Essen. Dann gehen Heribert und Susi mit Franz-Heinrich zu dem Kino. Der Film beginnt. Er heißt: "Zur Hölle und zurück. Die Abenteuer eines Mopedfahrers. In der Hauptrolle: Arnold Schwarzenegger." Gerade als Arnold mit seinem Moped mit 255 km/h durch die Hölleneingangstür rast, hört Heribert neben sich ein Röcheln. Franz-Heinrich fällt zu Boden. Er ist tot. Vergiftet! Heribert nimmt sein Handy und wählt 1-1-0. Der Herr Kommissar kommt sofort mit seinem BMW 740 tii und er untersucht den Fall. Der Kommissar befragt Heribert und Susi. Dann sagt er: "Der Mörder ist ....!" (Warum?)

Murder 2.

Susi and Heribert have a plan. They want to eat something and afterwards go to the movies. Susi and Heribert ride on Heribert's moped to Westby to Borgen's café. They enter the café and sit themselves at a table and order two Fanta and fries with mayonnaise and two sausages with mustard. In the café there are also Franz-Heinrich, Mr. Frosty Snowman, Mrs. Schorkelson, Gerhard Schröder, Angela Merkel and Alex. Franz-Heinrich orders tofu chips. Mr. Frosty Snowman is the cook. He appears coming out of the kitchen and signs a song: La la la dum dum da da and lala!" Gerhard Schröder and Mrs. Schnorkelson sing a yodeling duet. Mrs. Schnorkelson is the waitress. Angela Merkel and Alex talk (as always) about the good old days. Mrs. Schnorkelson brings the dishes first to Franz-Heinrich, then to Susi and Heribert. Then Heribert and Susi go together with Franz-Heinrich to the cinema. The movie starts. It is called: "To Hell and Back. The Adventures of a Moped Biker." Starring Arnold Schwarzenegger. Just when Arnold races with his moped at 255 km/h through the gates of hell, Heribert hears next to him the rattle of death. Franz-Heinrich sinks to the ground. He is dead. Poisoned! Heribert takes his mobile phone and dials 1-1-0. The Mr. Inspector arrives at once in his BMW 740 tii and he investigates the case. The inspector *interrogates Heribert and Susi. Then he says: "The murderer is ....! (Why?)*

Again, Herr Frosty Schneemann is the culprit. As the cook he has the possibility to poison Franz-Heinrich. However, an observant student might suggest that the waitress behaved suspiciously, and might be the culprit, which could lead to an interesting discussion among the students (in German, please!), possibly followed by a vote, to determine the culprit ...

Ein Mord 3
Susi und Heribert gehen zusammen aus. Sie wollen etwas einkaufen und danach in das Kino gehen. Susi und Heribert fahren mit Heribert's Motorschlitten zum Wal-Mart. Sie gehen in den Wal-Mart und kaufen zwei Fanta, Kartoffelchips, Orangen, Zitronen, Schnaps und zwei Würste mit Senf. In dem Wal-Mart sind auch Franz-Heinrich, Herr Frosty

Schneemann, Frau Schlau, Gerhard Blöd, Angela Stosceck und Alex. Franz-Heinrich lauert bei der Kasse. Herr Frosty Schneemann versteckt sich hinter den Winterjacken. Plötzlich kommt er hervor und singt ein Lied: "La la la dum dum da da und lala!" Gerhard Blöd und Frau Schlau lachen teuflisch. Frau Schlau arbeitet in der Kartoffelchipabteilung. Angela Stosceck und Alex schlafen an der Kasse. Dann bezahlen Heribert und Susi und gehen mit Franz-Heinrich zu dem Kino. Der Film beginnt. Heribert, Susi und Franz-Heinrich trinken Fanta und Franz-Heinrich ißt Kartoffelchips. Der Film heißt: "Das Chiplein. Ein Abenteuer in Liberty Pole." In den Hauptrollen: Ben C., Ben K., Alek R., und als bestbesetzte Nebenrolle Pat K.. Gerade als Ben mit seinem Ford mit 255 km/h über die Felder rast, hört Heribert neben sich ein Röcheln. Franz-Heinrich fällt zu Boden. Er ist tot. Vergiftet! Heribert nimmt sein Handy und wählt 1-1-0. Der Herr Kommissar kommt sofort mit seinem Moped. Der Kommissar befragt Heribert und Susi. Dann sagt er: "Der Mörder ist ………………..!" (Warum?)

Murder 3.
Susi and Heribert go out together. They want to go shopping and afterwards go to the movies. Susi and Heribert ride on Heribert's snow mobile to Wal-Mart. They enter the Wal-Mart and buy two Fanta, potato chips, oranges, lemons, schnapps and two sausages with mustard. Inside the Wal-Mart there are also Franz-Heinrich, Mr. Frosty Snowman, Mrs. Clever, Gerhard Stupid, Angela Stosceck and Alex. Franz-Heinrich lies in wait at the cash register. Mr. Frosty Snowman hides behind the winter jackets. Suddenly he emerges and sings a song: "La la la dum da da and lala!" Gerhard Stupid and Mrs. Clever laugh devilishly. Mrs. Clever works in the potato chip department. Angela Stosceck and Alex nap at the cash register. Then Heribert and Susi pay and go together with Franz-Heinrich to the cinema. The movie starts. Heribert, Susi and Franz-Heinrich

drink Fanta, and Franz-Heinrich eats potato chips. The movie is called: "The little chip. An adventure in Liberty Pole. Starring Ben C., Ben K., Alek R. and as best supporting actor Pat K." (All these are students in the class.) Just when Ben races across the fields in his Ford at 255 km/h, Heribert hears next to him the rattle of death. Franz-Heinrich sinks to the ground. He is dead. Poisoned! Heribert takes his mobile phone and dials 1-1-0. The Mr. Inspector arrives at once on his moped. The inspector interviews Heribert and Susi. Then he says: "The murderer is ....!" (Why?)

Frau Schlau, who works in the potato chip department, has laced the chips with poison, no?

Germans Are Funny

Chapter 2: *Das Gedicht (Poetry)*

Johann Wolfgang von Goethe (1749 – 1832)

Ah, poetry. Nothing is more beautiful and conveys the difficulties facing anyone, who wants to translate to or from a foreign language, than poetry. We have to deal with so much more than words. There is strong feeling, beauty, thoughts, images, rhyme and rhythm. Lucky are the students who can experience the beauty and simplicity, the depth and loftiness of *Goethe's* ultimate poem, "Wanderers Nachtlied":

Wanderers Nachtlied
Über allen Gipfeln ist Ruh,
In allen Wipfeln spürest du
Kaum einen Hauch;
Die Vögelein schweigen im Walde.
Warte nur! Balde
ruhest du auch.

Traveler's Evening Song
Peace on the mountain tops.
You sense in the tree-tops
Scarcely a breeze.
The birds in the woods hush their song -
Wait, before long,
You too will find ease.

Neither teacher nor student might ever come close to such simple profoundness, but all the more it should be an inspiration. It is an excellent idea to have the students from very early on, even while they are still struggling with very basic vocabulary, "play around" with words and poetry. Even playing with the sounds of the words without understanding the proper meaning is a great start! Students should be encouraged at all levels to always pay attention to and strive towards achieving poetry. Homework or in-class exercises of any kind can always find a crowning conclusion in the attempt to create a poetic piece, "ein Gedicht".

Following you will find a variety of simple poems. Many were created in class, or in connection with other subjects that the students were studying at the time, as this helps them to build a bridge between the foreign language class and the other subject classes like Chemistry, Physics, History, etc.

Gedicht 1
Klaus muß aus Haus raus.
Kein Schwein mein fein Wein dein nein Bein.
Ich nicht Wicht mich dich nicht dicht.
Wann kann Kahn Wahn Zahn Mann.
Blau Frau kau wau schau Bau.
Quatsch Matsch. Das Ende.

Poetry 1
Klaus must leave house.
No pig my fine vine your non leg.
I not gnome me you not tight.
When can boat madness tooth man.
Blue woman chew wow look building.
Nonsense muck. The end.

Gedicht 1 is such a poem where only the sound of the words is of importance, and to begin with this is a great way to help students, who think they have no poetry in them, or are shy about it, get started, and before they know it, they feel like poets.

Blaubeeren sind blau.
Blaubeeren sind blau.
Der Himmel ist grau.
Himbeeren sind rot.
Der Käfer ist tot.

Blueberries are blue.
Blueberries are blue.
The sky is gray.
Raspberries are red.
The beetle is dead.

Similarly you find here great simplicity, but with a funny – if melancholic – twist. The same poem is expanded upon, and then relates to learning the vocabulary necessary for botany ... drawing, ideally done by the students themselves, which identifies the various items in a garden and the vocabulary connected with each item and activity, should accompany this exercise.

58

Die Botanik oder Pflanzenkunde

Blaubeeren sind blau.
Der Himmel ist grau.
Himbeeren sind rot.
Der Käfer ist tot.

Ich liebe Karotten.
Ich hasse die Motten.
Ich trinke grünen Tee
Das tut mir nicht weh.

Wieviel Grünzeug ist auf dieser Welt?
Das Gemüse kostet viel Geld.
Der Gärtner ist ein netter Mann
Der alle Pflanzen gießen kann.

Botany or the Science of Plants

Blueberries are blue.
The sky is gray.
Raspberries are red.
The beetle is dead.

I love carrots.
I hate moths.
I drink green tea
Which doesn't hurt me.

How much green stuff is there in the world?
Vegetables cost a lot of money.
The gardener is a nice man
Who can water all the plants.

Learning about water, ecology, and regions of the world can all be connected by poetry that relates to each ...

Das Wasser

Das Wasser ist naß.
Hast du einen Paß?
Das Meer ist salzig.
Kennst du die Baltik?
Der Fluß fließt ins Meer.
Wo lebt der Bär?
Der Eisberg ist groß.
Was ist los?
Der See ist tief.
Deine Nase ist schief!
Der Regen fällt mir auf den Kopf.
Ich bin ein nasser Tropf.

Water

Water is wet.
Do you have a passport?
The sea is salty.
Do you know the Baltic (Sea)?
The river runs into the sea.
Where lives the bear?
The iceberg is big.
What's going on?
The lake is deep.
Your nose is crooked!
Rain falls on my head.
I am a wet little gnome.

... or to a science course like chemistry ...

Die Chemie
Die Chemie, die Chemie,
Die versteh' ich nie!
Sauerstoff und Wasserstoff,
Das gibt's nicht auf mein' Bauernhof.
Schwefelsäure und Dynamit,
Da komm ich nicht mit.
Wieviel Stickstoff ist im Haus?
Frage doch die Maus!
Wo ist denn H 2 O?
Vielleicht in meinem Klo.
Was mach' ich mit Kohlendioxid?
Ich frage meinen Freund Piet.
Die Luft ist ein Gas, das Wasser ist flüssig,
Der Stein ist hart und kalt und nicht schlüssig.
Aber die Chemie, die Chemie,
Die versteh' ich nie!

Chemistry
Chemistry, chemistry
I don't understand it!
Oxygen and Hydrogen,
We don't have such on our farm.
C2O and dynamite,
I don't get it.
How much Nitrogen is in my house?
Ask the mouse!
Where is H2O?
Perhaps in the toilet.
What do I do with carbon dioxide?
I ask my friend Piet.
The air is gaseous, the water is fluid,
The stone is hard and cold and not making sense.
But chemistry, chemistry,
I don't understand it!

Periodic Table of the Elements

Groups: 1 IA, 2 IIA, 13 IIIA, 14 IVA, 15 VA, 16 VIA, 17 VIIA, 18 VIIIA

1 H Hydrogen 1.00794
2 He Helium 4.002602
3 Li Lithium 6.941
4 Be Beryllium 9.012182
5 B Boron 10.811
6 C Carbon 12.0107
7 N Nitrogen 14.00674
8 O Oxygen 15.9994
9 F Fluorine 18.9984032
10 Ne Neon 20.1797
11 Na Sodium 22.989770
12 Mg Magnesium 24.3050
13 Al Aluminum 26.981539
14 Si Silicon 28.0855
15 P Phosphorus 30.973761
16 S Sulfur 32.066
17 Cl Chlorine 35.4527
18 Ar Argon 39.948
19 K Potassium 39.0983
20 Ca Calcium 40.078
21 Sc
22–30 Übergangsmetalle
30 Zn
31 Ga Gallium 69.723
32 Ge Germanium 72.64
33 As Arsenic 74.92160
34 Se Selenium 78.96
35 Br Bromine 79.904
36 Kr Krypton 83.798
37 Rb Rubidium 85.4678
38 Sr Strontium 87.62
39 Y Übergangsmetalle
48 Cd
49 In Indium 114.818
50 Sn Tin 118.710
51 Sb Antimony 121.760
52 Te Tellurium 127.60
53 I Iodine 126.90447
54 Xe Xenon 131.293
55 Cs Cesium 132.90545
56 Ba Barium 137.327
57 La Übergangsmetalle / Lanthaniden
58 Ce
71 Lu
80 Hg
81 Tl Thallium 204.3833
82 Pb Lead 207.2
83 Bi Bismuth 208.98038
84 Po Polonium (209)
85 At Astatine (210)
86 Rn Radon (222)
87 Fr Francium (223)
88 Ra Radium (226)
89 Ac Übergangsmetalle / Actiniden
90 Th
103 Lr
112 Uub

Legend:
Alkalimetalle
Erdalkalimetalle
Metalle
Übergangsmetalle
Nichtmetalle
Edelgase

Biographies of poets should be brought to the students on a regular basis. More advanced students should be asked to research a poet, and prepare a presentation about the same to the class or to the teacher, including a basic biography, some artwork, and naturally a number of the poems by the poet, both in the original version and translations or interpretations by the student.

Die Tramödie
Eine Komödie ist keine Tragödie
Und eine Tragödie ist keine Komödie
Aber die Tragödie ist vielleicht komisch
Und die Komödie sogar tragisch
Der Herr Goethe kennt beide
Der Herr Schiller liebt seine
Aber Novalis liebt nur eine
Ist das tragisch oder komisch?

The Tragicomedy
A comedy is not a tragedy
And a tragedy is not a comedy
But the tragedy is perhaps comically
And the comedy even tragically
Mr. Goethe knows both
Mr. Schiller loves his
But Novalis loves only the one
Is that tragic or comic?

Novalis (Georg Friedrich Freiherr von Hardenberg, 1772 – 1801)

Psychology, love, and soul searching are all subjects of great interest to the students of this age (grade 6 – 12). Poetry is a wonderful way to work with the concepts that the students learn about in other classes and relate it to their German class experience.

Mein süßer kleiner Käfer
My sweet little bug

Komm in meine Arme
Come into my arms

Was? Du willst nicht?
What? You don't want to?

Wir haben halt kein Karma!
Well – we don't have karma!

Die Psychologie
Die Psychologie
Die versteh ich nie
Freud ist nicht lustig
Jung ist zu alt
Skinner viel zu mickrig
Und Pavlov 'ne Maus
Mein Schatten ist wichtig
Mein Über-Ich richtig
Und Herr Steiner
vielschichtig
Die Sterne bestimmen
Die Planeten schwimmen
Im Ozean der Nacht
Meine Seele gehört mir
Und ich verkauf' sie nicht dir!

Psychology
Psychology
I never understand it
Freud is not funny
Jung is too old
Skinner way too skinny
And Pavlov a mouse
My shadow is important
My Super-Ego is right
And Mr. Steiner
multi-layered
The stars determine
The planets swim
In the ocean of the night
My soul belongs to me
And I won't sell it to you!

DIE PSYCHOLOGIE

Die Psychologie
Die versteh ich nie
Freud ist nicht lustig
Jung ist zu alt
Skinner viel zu mickrig
Und Pawlov 'ne Maus
Mein Schatten ist wichtig
Mein Über-'Ich richtig
Und Herr Steiner vielschichtig
Die Sterne bestimmen
Die Planeten schwimmen
Im Ozean der Nacht
Meine Seele gehört mir
Und ich verkauf' sie nicht dir!

The psychology
That I never understand
Freud isn't funny
Jung is to old
Skinner is to skinny
And Pawlov is a mouse
My shadow is important
My super-ego is right
And Mr. Steiner is multi-layered
The stars decide
The planets swim
In the ocean of the night
My soul belong to me
And I don't sell it to you!

Revolutionary upheaval in all its forms and manifestations is another pastime of the healthy teenager.

Die Revolution

Am Montag haben wir 'ne Revolution
Der Kaiser, Tsar, und Kapitän muß weg
Wir kämpfen, schießen, köpfen

Alles Alte in den Dreck!
Neue Führer, neue Lieder
Doch aufgepaßt! Schon wieder –
Kommen neue Könige daher

Gestern Revoluzzer, heute Herren,
Und morgen? Vielleicht ein Neuer,
Vielleicht ein Ungeheuer.

Revolution

On Monday we'll have a revolution
The emperor, Czar, and captain have to go
We fight, shoot, behead

Everything of old into the dirt!
New leaders, new songs
But watch out! Already again –
New kings appear.

Yesterday's revolutionaries are today's masters,
And tomorrow? Perhaps a new one,
Perhaps a monster.

Germans Are Funny

Chapter 3: *Im Restaurant (Restaurant)*

We all need to eat! While visiting a foreign country we will sooner or later land up in a café or restaurant, and will be faced with the prospect of ordering food. Now we might do that the way I did when visiting Bulgaria: Not knowing more than 3 words of the language spoken there, I listened to the waiter explaining the choices for dinner, by counting them out with the help of his fingers. I simply ordered "ring finger", and it turned out to be fine! Perhaps a better way is to practice ordering in a restaurant in German many times before the event actually happens. The students like this activity very much, and one can role play this event in many different ways. The students might be customers, or waiters, or both, or take turns. We might actually go as far as preparing meals and serving them only to those who are able to order! It is also important to make sure that all stay in character. Perhaps they can even get a feel for the cultural differences expressed in the seeming lack of interest in commerce in the German culture: When it comes to serving customers or letting them pay for their food – there is always a bit of a wait involved, and nobody ever gets rushed to leave or order something else.

And don't forget the drawings and pictures of restaurant and café scenes ...

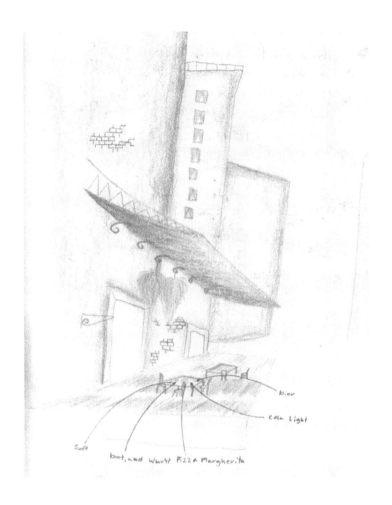

But most important is of course the menu, the "Speisekarte". It is a good idea to have a few of these available, and the more we make them close to a real *Speisekarte* the better it will be. Students may work on an artistic creation, or we can provide a simplified version of an actual menu that we have brought home from our last trip to Germany, or we need to make one up. And don't forget the humor.

PIZZERIA ROMA

Mit Lieferservice

Wir liefern Frei Haus!

Pizza (klein, mittel, oder groß)

Bitte wählen Sie von den folgenden Zutaten:
- ❏ Käse
- ❏ Salami
- ❏ Thunfisch
- ❏ Paprika
- ❏ Zwiebeln
- ❏ Knoblauch
- ❏ Artischockenherzen
- ❏ Sauerkraut
- ❏ Oliven
- ❏ Motoröl (SAE 30)
- ❏ Pilze

Pasta
- ❏ Spaghetti mit Tomatensoße
- ❏ Spaghetti mit Sahnesoße und Schinken
- ❏ Spaghetti mit vier Käsesorten
- ❏ Bandnudeln mit Schinken und Zwiebeln
- ❏ Bandnudeln ohne alles
- ❏ Lasagne mit Paprika und Hackfleisch
- ❏ Lasagne mit Äpfeln und Sojakäse
- ❏ Lasagne mit Sahnesoße und Wurst

Fleischgerichte

- ☐ Wienerschnitzel mit Pommes Frites
- ☐ Sauerbraten nach Art des Hauses
- ☐ Schweinebauch mit Pilzen
- ☐ Gebratenes Huhn mit Zwiebelringen
- ☐ Döner Kebab mit Knoblauchsoße (scharf)
- ☐ Tote Maus mit Ketchup
- ☐ Sojawurst mit Grünkern und Gemüse

Getränkekarte

Alkoholfrei
- ☐ Cola
- ☐ Spezi
- ☐ Limonade
- ☐ Apfelsaft
- ☐ Orangensaft
- ☐ Mangosaft mit Kirschen

Heiße Getränke
- ☐ Kaffee
- ☐ Kaffee mit Schlagsahne
- ☐ Kinderkaffee (ohne Kaffein)
- ☐ Schwarzer Tee
- ☐ Kräutertee
- ☐ Grüner Tee
- ☐ Tee mit Rum
- ☐ Espresso
- ☐ Café coretto (Espresso mit Grappa)
- ☐ Cappucino

Bier
- ☐ Helles
- ☐ Dunkles
- ☐ Weizenbier
- ☐ Pils
- ☐ Idiotenbier

Wein
- ☐ Rot
- ☐ Weiß
- ☐ Grüne Flasche

Mit Lieferservice

Wir liefern Frei Haus!

Pizza (small, medium, large)

Please chose from the following ingredients:
- ❑ Cheese
- ❑ Salami
- ❑ Tuna
- ❑ Peppers
- ❑ Onions
- ❑ Garlic
- ❑ Artichoke hearts
- ❑ Sour kraut
- ❑ Olives
- ❑ Motor oil (SAE 30)
- ❑ Mushrooms

Pasta
- ❑ Spaghetti with tomato sauce
- ❑ Spaghetti Alfredo with ham
- ❑ Spaghetti with four cheeses
- ❑ Fettucine with ham and onions
- ❑ Fettucine with nothing
- ❑ Lasagne with peppers and hamburger
- ❑ Lasagne with apples and soy cheese
- ❑ Lasagne Alfredo with sausage

Meat dishes

- Wienerschnitzel with fries
- Sauerbraten (house specialty)
- Pig stomach with mushrooms
- Grilled chicken with onion rings
- Döner Kebab with garlic sauce (hot)
- Dead mouse with ketchup
- Soy sausage with Grünkern and vegetables

Beverages

Non-alcoholic
- Cola
- Spezi
- Lemonade
- Apple juice
- Orange juice
- Mango juice with cherries

Hot beverages
- Coffee
- Coffee with cream
- Children's coffee (decaffeinated)
- Black tea
- Herbal tea
- Green tea
- Tea with rum
- Espresso
- Café coretto (Espresso with Grappa)
- Cappucino

Beer
- Light
- Dark
- Wheat beer
- Pilsener
- Idiot's beer

Vine
- Red
- White
- Green bottle

No matter what your own convictions are concerning alcohol, one should never miss the opportunity to talk about it. The cultural differences and sensibilities should be addressed and the fact that alcohol is available to minors in many cultures, including the German culture, should not be ignored, but rather used to stimulate a lively discussion about the pros and cons of more restrictive and less restrictive approaches to the dangers posed by alcohol.

Speisekarte

Paprikacremesuppe mit Bärlauchpesto ....€ 3,60
Red pepper cream soup with bears' garlic pesto

Frühlings-Blattsalatemit mariniertem Fetakäse, getrockneten Tomaten und schwarzen Oliven.. € 8,50
Spring salad with marinated feta cheese, dried tomatoes and black olives

Gebratene Hähnchenbrust auf Gnocchi in Kräutersauce mit Bärlauch und geriebenem Parmesan................................. € 9,70
Fried chicken breast with gnocchi, herb sauce with bears' garlic and shredded parmesan

Geschnetzeltes vom Känguruhfilet in Rotweinsauce mit sautierten Waldpilzen und Basmatireis ....€ 11,50
Slices of kangaroo filet with red wine sauce, sautéed mushrooms and basmati rice

Gegrillte Tranchen vom Lachs auf Schalotten-Weißweinsauce mit Gemüsebouquet und Kräuterkartoffeln ....€ 9,90
Grilled salmon with shallot white wine sauce, vegetables and herb potatoes

Knackiges Wokgemüse mit gebratenen Putenbruststreifen in Ingwer-Austernsauce und Duftreis ....€ 10,80
Crispy vegetables "Thai style " with slices of turkey breast, ginger-oyster sauce and steamed rice

Dessert der Woche

Frische marinierte Erdbeeren mit Bourbon-Vanilleeis....€ 5,30
Fresh marinated strawberries with Bourbon vanilla ice cream

Speisekarte

Schwein vom Grill ....€ 6,20
mit Knödel und Salat

Bauernschmaus....................€ 6,20

Schweineschnitzl.................€ 5,20
mit Salat

Bratwürste ....€ 2,50
mit Senf und Gebäck

Weitwieser Bauernsalat.......€ 4,80

Die Speisen stammen aus unserem
kontrolliert biologischen Betrieb

Guten Appetit
wünscht Familie Stark

Germans Are Funny

Chapter 4: *Das Wetter (Weather)*

Talk about the weather. This subject has many aspects to it, and it is always available. One possibility is to start each session with sharing a current weather report by leading the students to simply look out the window and describe what they are able to observe. A thermometer attached to the outside of the classroom window is a very helpful piece of equipment. Other equipment could be used as it is available. Weather reports from a German-speaking country are an excellent source for presentations, especially when used in a way mimicking a TV or radio weatherman. One can also make this into an exercise of phenomenological scientific observation by keeping a daily journal recording the weather phenomena as they present themselves to the naked eye observation.

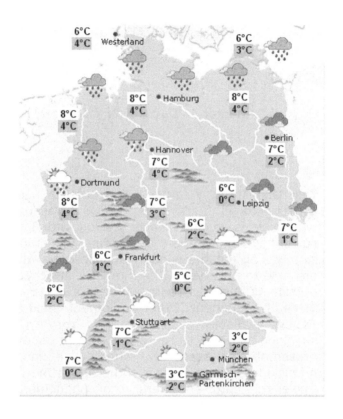

A weather map is essential to have available, but can be easily obtained from online sources. You may want to print out a large map, possibly "stitching" together for pages to form one large poster, or you can hand out individual maps to each student, or – as behooves the good Waldorf educator – you draw a beautiful weather map on large poster board, either by yourself, or as an activity to be done together with the students. Once the map is there, you can use it for many exercises. Following you will find some suggestions:

Bitte übersetzen: Deutschland heute: Heute scheint dank Hoch RONALD größtenteils die Sonne, und es bleibt weitgehend trocken. Im äußersten Westen und Südwesten, sowie im Allgäu und in den Bayrischen Alpen tauchen durch Tief BIANKA aber tagsüber zeitweise Schauer oder örtlich auch Gewitter auf. Der Wind weht meist schwach bis mäßig, an den Küsten und im Nordosten frisch, und in Böen stark, vorwiegend aus östlichen Richtungen.

Bitte beantworten: Scheint in Frankfurt die Sonne? Wo regnet es? Ist es warm in Westerland? Kannst du in der Nordsee schwimmen gehen? Gibt es im Bayrischen Wald Bären?

Please translate: Germany today: Today thanks to high pressure system RONALD mostly sunny, and dry. In the far West and Southwest, also in the Allgäu and the Bavarian Alps – because of the low pressure system BIANKA – a few showers and local thunderstorms. Wind is weak to medium, at the coasts fresh, with some strong gusts, predominately out of the East.

Please answer: Does the sun shine in Frankfurt? Where does it rain? Is it warm in Westerland? Can you go swimming in the North Sea? Are there bears in the Bavarian forest?

Bitte komplettieren

Heute ist _____.
Das _____ in Westby ist heute
_____. Warum ist Borgen's Café
_____? Der Feuerwehrhauptmann
von Westby schaut zu _____ und
schreit: "_____!" Die
Temperatur ist unter _____ und der Wind
_____. _____ lieben Schnee und
_____ aber nicht _____. Das Taxi
fährt durch _____; plötzlich ist
_____. Ein Regenbogen ist
_____. Ich _____ den
Regenbogen und auch _____. Der Himmel
_____ wolkenlos. Mein Regenschirm ist
_____ und _____. Wo ist
_____ heute? Jetzt kommt Susi im
Amishtaxi aus _____. Susi hat
_____ und geht _____. Susi schreit:
"Heribert _____! Aber das Amishtaxi
_____. Heribert rennt _____. Das
Gewitter kommt mit _____. Susi _____
zu Borgen's Café und bestellt _____. Herr
Frosty Schneemann sagt: "_____".
Plötzlich ist das _____ schwül. Die
_____ steigt auf 35 ° C. Ein Wolkenbruch,
ein Orkan, und ein Wirbelwind _____ den
Schnee in Westby. Das ist _____. Susi geht
nach _____.

Please complete

Today is _____.
The _____ in Westby is today
_____. Why ist Borgen's Café
_____? The fire brigade captain of
Westby looks at _____ and yells:
"_____!" The temperature is
below _____ and the wind _____.

86

_____ love snow and _____ but not _____. The taxi drives through _____; suddenly there is _____. A rainbow is _____. I _____ the rainbow and also _____. The sky _____ cloudless. My umbrella is _____ and _____. Where is _____ today? There arrives Susi in the Amish taxi from _____. Susi has _____ and goes to _____. Susi yells: "Heribert _____! But the Amish taxi _____. Heribert races _____. The thunderstorm comes with _____. Susi _____ to Borgen's café and orders _____. Mr. Frosty Snowman says: "_____". Suddenly the _____ is muggy. The _____ rises to 35 ° C. A cloud burst, a hurricane, and a tornado _____ the snow in Westby. That is _____. Susi goes to _____.

87

Übersetzen und die Fragen beantworten

"Heribert" bringt viel Niederschlag

Tief "Heribert" sorgt in den kommenden Wochen für viel Niederschlag in Deutschland. Nach einem winterlichen Orkan mit sehr viel Schneefall bis in die Täler von Hamburg und München, steigen die Temperaturen zum Wochenende bis auf +30 Grad Celcius. "Diese abwechselnd warmen und kalten Luftmassen lassen dem Winter einfach keine Chance", meinte Susi vom Wetterdienst in Berlin. (Frage: "Was ist der Wetterdienst?")

Translate and answer the questions

"Heribert" brings lots of precipitation

Low pressure system "Heribert" will provide Germany in the coming weeks with lots of precipitation. Following a winterly hurricane with lots of snow all the way to the valleys of Hamburg and Munich, the temperatures will climb before the weekend to +30 degrees Celsius. "These changing warm and cold air masses give winter no chance," suggests Susi from the weather service in Berlin. (Question: "What is the weather service?")

Übersetzen und die Fragen beantworten

Kältewelle beschert USA eisige Temperaturen

Eine Kältewelle aus Kanada hat den Nordosten der USA in einen eisigen Würgegriff genommen. Mit minus 48 Grad wurden in der Stadt Liberty Pole im US-Bundesstaat Wisconsin Extremtemperaturen nahe dem Rekordtief von 1621 gemessen, berichteten Studenten von der ... Schule. Zwischen Viroqua und La Crosse fielen 14 Kühe und 23 Schweine tot aus einem Hühnerstall. (Frage: "Warum?")

Translate and answer the questions

Cold front delivers ice temperatures to the USA
A cold front from Canada has leveled an icy grip on the northeast of the USA. Students from the … school report that extreme temperatures of minus 48 degrees were measured in the city of Liberty Pole in the US federal state of Wisconsin, which is close to the record low of 1621. Between Viroqua and La Crosse 14 cows and 23 pigs fell from a chicken coop – dead. (Question: Why?)

The technique of leading the students through the 3 steps of creating a "good" translation, should be encouraged at all times. The following exercise exemplifies the method. Step 1: Read the text and get a feeling for the content and context, possibly giving or - for advanced students – having the students give a summary of the text. Step 2: A literal, word for word translation is being created by the students, possibly with help. Step 3: The students re-translate the literal translation into "good" English.

Wetterbericht (Original):
Deutschland heute: Heute bleibt es häufig trüb, und vor allem im Norden und Osten fällt ab und zu Regen oder Sprühregen. Im Südosten fällt anfangs noch Glatteisregen oder Schnee. Hier kann es weiterhin glatt sein! Lediglich auf der Ostseite der Mittelgebirge zeigen sich ab und zu Wolkenlücken. Im Süden bläßt ein schwacher bis mäßiger, im Norden ein frischer bis starker Wind aus West. An den Küsten und in den Höhenlagen der Mittelgebirge kommt es zu Sturmböen zwischen 60 und 100 km/h.

Weather Report (Literal Translation):
Germany today: Today stays it mostly dreary, and before all in North and East falls on and off rain or drizzle. In the Southeast falls at first still freezing drizzle or snow. Here can it continuously slippery be! Only at the east side of the "Mittelgebirge" show itself on and off gaps in the cloud cover. In South blows a weak to medium, in North a fresh to strong wind from West. On the coast and in the higher elevations of the "Mittelgebirge" comes it to storm gusts between 60 and 100 km/h.

Weather Report (Good Translation):
Germany today: Today will be a dreary day. Especially in the North and East we will occasionally see some rain or drizzle. During the morning hours we will experience in the Southeast still some freezing rain or snow. Careful! It might be icy! Only on the eastern side of the Mittelgebirge we will have some blue sky peaking through the clouds. In the South we will experience weak to mild wind. In the North however there will be a fresh and sometimes strong wind coming out of the West. At the coast and in the higher elevations of the Mittelgebirge, there will even be some storm gusts with wind speeds between 60 and 100 km/h.

A more basic exercise ...

Deutschland heute: Schneewolken ziehen von Tschechien und Österreich herein. So schneit es vor allem in Süddeutschland, in Brandenburg, Thüringen und Sachsen. Sonst gibt es nur gelegentlich Schneeschauer. Der Wind weht im Süden schwach bis mäßig, im Norden und in den Mittelgebirgen auch frisch bis stark aus nördlichen Richtungen.

Bitte den Text übersetzen und die genannten Orte auf der Karte markieren

Deutschland today: Snow clouds pull in from the Czech Republic and Austria. Therefore it will snow especially in Southern Germany, Brandenburg, Thüringen and Sachsen. Otherwise only occasional snow showers. Wind will be weak to mild in the South, in the North and in the Mittelgebirge also fresh to strong out of the North.

Translate text, and indicate the locations mentioned in the text on the map

Germans Are Funny

Chapter 5: *Das Rätsel (Riddles)*

Crossword puzzles and similar exercises not only train the mind in finding solutions within a given roster, but also train the faculties of recognizing words, thereby training one of the higher senses, the "word sense". And they are fun! The riddles can either be prepared by the teacher, or by advanced students for beginning students, or by the students for each other. A simple grit can be provided by using pen and ruler, or using the electronic version with a spreadsheet program, which might especially appeal to the "techno-wizards" in your class. Electronic versions have the advantage that they can easily be adapted to new creations, corrections, and updates. Another possibility suitable for a small group of students (4 or less) is the use of the famous board game "Scrabble" of which there exists a German version. You can order this on amazon.de or ask your relatives in Germany to send one for Christmas. With larger groups of students you can also play a sort of blackboard Scrabble. To do this you simply start with a long word, written in capital letters on the blackboard, and then solicit words that connect Scrabble-style to the given word on the blackboard, until you end up with a nice roster of words.

Here is a simple, home-made crossword puzzle.

KREUZWORTRÄTSEL

1 who
2 across: bird down: full
3 one
4 across: mountain down: German capital
5 you live in it
6 a certain school
6A stupid
7 rope
8 male farm bird does not lay eggs
9 duck
10 how many days are there in a week?
11 even, smooth

12 idea
13 aunt
14 a Scandinavian country
15 pronoun
16 no
17 you drive with it
18 article
19 concerning multiple nations. global

And the solution …

K R E U Z W O R T R Ä T S E L

W
E
B E R G V O G E L
I
H E O N
W A L D O R F S C H U L E S I E B E N
U O L E A N B I
S O I I H T A N T E I N
F I N N L A N D E N F
C E U E A
H I N T E R N A T I O N A L
N O L

copyright Conrad Rehbach

97

In this example the task is to find the words "hidden" on the page.

H	E	T	T	U	J	H	N	L	K	S	S	S	P	O	P
Q	E	Y	U	N	M	K	L	C	E	L	S	I	U	S	L
P	M	R	Y	F	N	V	D	F	G	H	J	K	R	U	R
M	U	M	I	X	E	N	U	T	F	D	D	Z	T	S	H
O	G	I	V	B	A	C	K	E	N	M	K	E	W	I	L
J	U	N	E	K	E	K	S	E	V	G	A	A	L	M	N
A	D	U	T	R	V	J	E	L	K	D	R	S	U	R	N
M	N	T	R	F	C	X	T	Y	S	A	H	N	E	N	M
O	R	E	Y	W	W	B	D	O	V	X	W	K	L	B	N
R	E	N	T	N	D	T	D	N	D	A	C	K	J	L	N
U	Y	T	H	B	V	E	Y	G	F	U	M	K	P	O	O
K	A	S	S	U	P	O	P	Q	Z	U	T	A	T	E	N
A	O	L	L	O	N	M	Y	E	C	H	E	U	T	R	D
F	P	P	M	E	H	L	L	U	I	H	I	D	B	L	M
F	O	O	F	G	K	L	B	N	M	G	G	U	T	F	D
E	I	N	M	E	I	E	R	M	N	G	N	L	P	B	H
E	I	O	N	N	V	C	K	J	M	E	E	W	U	I	J
O	P	N	A	F	C	U	Z	X	L	L	H	M	N	V	F
P	O	V	B	H	S	D	Y	L	N	K	O	P	D	F	H
R	T	N	Z	H	J	K	O	B	H	J	N	K	M	F	Y
T	Y	S	U	P	E	R	M	A	R	K	T	N	K	H	G
U	H	D	C	M	N	M	B	C	U	J	R	R	T	F	N
U	B	N	K	R	T	U	H	K	N	B	M	E	Y	R	T
E	F	F	E	R	W	M	C	P	I	T	H	S	I	O	P
P	B	K	R	F	G	H	G	U	F	D	R	D	F	S	J
W	E	R	T	E	R	T	R	L	Y	H	B	N	X	Z	E
I	K	L	N	M	E	R	D	V	L	L	K	N	M	V	C
N	B	B	A	C	K	O	F	E	N	U	J	H	D	F	R
T	G	D	G	E	R	T	W	R	Q	B	J	K	L	F	S

HERIBERT   CELSIUS   KREISE   BACKOFEN   MIXEN   BACKEN   KEKSE   MOPED

SUPERMARKT   MEHL   ZUCKER   BACKPULVER   VANILLEZUCKER   EIER

SAHNE   ZUTATEN   TEIG   KREISE   KAFFEE   MINUTEN   ROLLEN

With the solution pictured below …

H													
	E						C	E	L	S	I	U	S
		R										U	
		M	I	X	E	N						S	
		I	B	A	C	K	E	N				I	
		N	K	E	K	S	E						
		U			R							R	
		T			T		S	A	H	N	E		
		E								K			
		N			D				C				
				E				U					
K			P				Z	U	T	A	T	E	N
A			O		E			E					
F		M	E	H	L	L		I					
F			L					G					
E		E	I	E	R			N					
E		N					E						
		A				L							
	V					L							
	Z				O	B							
	S	U	P	E	R	M	A	R	K	T			
	C					C		R					
	K					K			E				
	E					P				I			
	R					U					S		
						L							E
						V							
	B	A	C	K	O	F	E	N					
						R							

HERIBERT   CELSIUS   KREISE   BACKOFEN   MIXEN   BACKEN   KEKSE   MOPED

SUPERMARKT   MEHL   ZUCKER   BACKPULVER   VANILLEZUCKER   EIER

SAHNE   ZUTATEN   TEIG   KREISE   KAFFEE   MINUTEN   ROLLEN

And ...

D	U	M	M	K	O	P	F	W	V	G	Q	O	J	O	A
R	E	U	E	I	R	B	N	F	U	S	S	B	A	L	L
U	I	U	U	H	K	N	E	C	B	Y	P	F	N	V	A
J	K	K	T	S	A	S	R	Y	T	L	O	M	M	K	N
G	J	D	E	S	N	D	S	D	W	V	R	F	R	I	G
P	O	L	R	I	C	H	A	R	D	E	T	P	O	L	W
L	K	P	E	E	R	H	E	G	B	S	V	T	N	E	E
N	H	J	I	B	T	E	E	H	J	T	E	R	T	M	I
V	G	Y	T	E	B	N	M	R	R	E	R	T	E	I	L
U	S	O	L	N	B	F	D	S	A	R	E	X	C	B	I
S	P	I	E	G	E	L	E	I	E	R	I	V	H	L	G
H	I	H	J	U	V	J	K	O	V	O	N	Y	I	I	T
I	N	I	Y	U	B	E	N	O	M	L	L	H	M	T	T
O	N	H	G	N	B	C	R	S	D	S	G	T	B	Z	T
W	R	T	Y	E	R	H	E	B	R	T	Y	F	E	A	K
T	A	E	E	Y	E	J	G	O	O	V	C	R	E	B	E
B	D	S	Y	R	R	D	S	O	V	T	C	X	R	L	Z
G	H	J	S	K	L	M	N	T	H	F	E	I	M	E	R
W	T	A	T	E	D	D	B	M	B	T	T	N	A	I	T
A	G	A	D	B	R	A	N	Z	I	G	J	G	R	T	K
E	N	B	C	R	C	V	D	F	T	B	B	U	M	E	U
J	H	Y	U	A	D	V	C	H	E	R	I	B	E	R	T
P	O	L	I	Z	E	I	A	U	T	O	E	E	L	W	R
W	P	O	U	Z	T	T	U	N	L	S	J	K	A	G	R
W	E	R	R	I	Y	H	G	D	F	E	V	B	D	M	J
I	L	V	B	A	N	U	I	E	I	N	R	R	E	T	Y
J	K	L	J	K	V	B	V	O	D	F	T	Y	E	V	M
D	O	N	N	E	R	S	C	H	L	A	G	U	M	M	J
A	L	K	J	R	E	D	C	R	V	B	N	T	Y	I	O

100

Solution …

D	U	M	M	K	O	P	F							
	E		E	R			F	U	S	S	B	A	L	L
		U	U	K					Y	P				A
			T	A					L	O				N
			E	S	N				V	R				G
			R	I	C	H	A	R	D	E	T			W
			E	E		H			S	V			E	E
			I	B			E		T	E		T		I
				E				R	E	R	T			L
	S			N					R	E			B	I
S	P	I	E	G	E	L	E	I	E	R	I	H	L	G
	I				V				V		N	I	I	
	N				E			O				M	T	
	N					R						B	Z	
W	R					H		B				E	A	
	A			E				O	O		R	E	B	E
	D	S	R					O		T		R	L	
		S	R				T			E	I	M	E	R
	A		E								N	A	I	
	G			R	A	N	Z	I	G			R	T	
E			R									M	E	
	A						H	E	R	I	B	E	R	T
P	O	L	I	Z	E	I	A	U	T	O		L		
		Z						N	S			A		
		I						D	E			D		
		A						E	N			E		
								O						
D	O	N	N	E	R	S	C	H	L	A	G			
								R						

101

This is an example of a different riddle. The words in the top row are listed again in the bottom row, but now the letters are sorted alphabetically. The students receive only the lower row of letters and then have the task to re-arrange the letters in such fashion that they recognize and find the words in their original state.

s	k	h	s	k	s	s	h	s
c	a	a	p	a	o	p	e	c
h	r	m	e	f	j	i	r	h
o	t	m	i	f	a	e	i	m
k	o	e	s	e	b	g	n	a
o	f	l	e	e	u	e	g	c
l	f	f	k		r	l		k
a	e	l	a		g	e		h
d	l	e	r		e	i		a
e	b	i	t		r			f
	r	s	e					t
	e	c						
	i	h						

a	a	a	a	a	a	e	e	a
c	b	c	e	e	e	e	g	a
d	e	e	e	e	b	e	h	c
e	e	e	e	e	e	g	i	c
h	e	e	i	f	g	i	n	f
k	f	f	k	f	j	i	r	h
l	f	h	p	k	o	l		h
o	i	h	r		r	p		k
o	k	i	s		r	s		m
s	l	l	s		s			s
	o	l	t		u			t
	r	m						
	r	m						
	t	s						

102

Germans Are Funny

Chapter 6: *Wo bin ich? (Where am I?)*

Real men do not ask for directions. Why? Because they are unable to follow directions! Nevertheless, asking and giving directions is – as we know – one of the activities we cannot do without, especially when we go to foreign places, and I don't mean the "foreign" ATM machine on the other side of town, but real foreign lands. It is best to start with activities that involve the immediate surroundings, and, after having introduced the basic vocabulary for this task, to have the students learn to give directions to the poor stranger that got lost right outside the school building (or whichever place one is in). It is interesting in itself to find out, who of the students, actually knows, where the bank, the post

office, the restaurant, the gas station, supermarket, etc., actually are, besides being able to give directions to and from one's own house. Next, the students should be able to give and ask for directions around the home town, and it is a good idea to make a few maps, either individually or as a group project. For instance, to make a huge map of one's home town, or the city blocks, where the school is situated, including all the landmarks like park, bank, grocery store, mini golf place, swimming pool, etc. The side of a refrigerator card board box is a good size poster board to use.

Basic Vocabulary and expressions:

Entschuldigung ...
Excuse me ...

Wie komme ich nach ... bis nach ...
How do I get to ... up to ...

zu dem = zum

to (the)

Nehmen Sie ... bis ...
Take ... to ...

Gehen Sie ...
Go ...

Fahren Sie ...
Drive ...

Dann nehmen Sie ... bis ...
Then take ... until ...

links
left

rechts
right

geradeaus
straight ahead

gegenüber
opposite

Immer der Nase nach
Follow your nose

(Strassen)ecke
street corner

Kreuzung (von)
crossroads

Hausnummer
street address

Hauptstrasse
Main Street

Tankstelle
Gas station

Kino
Movie theater

Post
Post office

Bücherei
Library

Supermarkt
Supermarket

Restaurant
Restaurant

Schwimmbad
Swimming pool

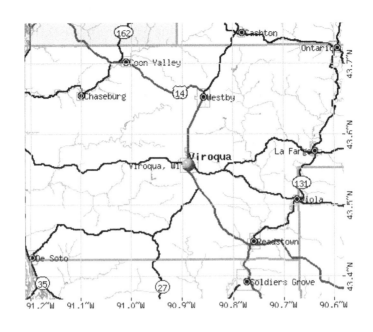

Following a simple map of a town in Wisconsin and questions that the students need to answer using their knowledge of where the localities described might be, and practicing "giving directions". The exercises can be done individually in writing, or in small groups, and/or as question and answer either between teacher and students or between more advanced students and beginners.

Bitte übersetzen und die Lokalitäten auf der Karte anzeigen.
Translate and indicate the locations on the map.

1. Wo ist das Landmark Center? Where is the Landmark Center?
2. Wo ist die Bibliothek? Where is the library?
3. Wo ist das Café namens Common Ground? Where is the café called Common Ground?
4. Wo ist das Café namens Driftless Cafe? Where is the cafe called Driftless Cafe?
5. Wo ist das Postamt? Where is the post office?
6. Wo ist der Drogeriemarkt namens Walgreens? Where is the pharmacy called Walgreens?
7. Wo ist der Radio Shack? Where is the Radio Shack?
8. Wo ist Itas Haus? Where is Ita's house?
9. Wo ist Kristens Haus? Where is Kristen's house?
10. Wo ist Heriberts Moped? Where is Heribert's moped?
11. Wo ist das Kino? Where is the movie theater?
12. Wo ist der "Family Dollar" Supermarkt? Where is the "Family Dollar" supermarket?
13. Wo ist der Friedhof? Where is the cemetery?

Wie komme ich von dem Landmark Center zu dem Common Ground?
How do I get from the Landmark Center to the Common Ground?

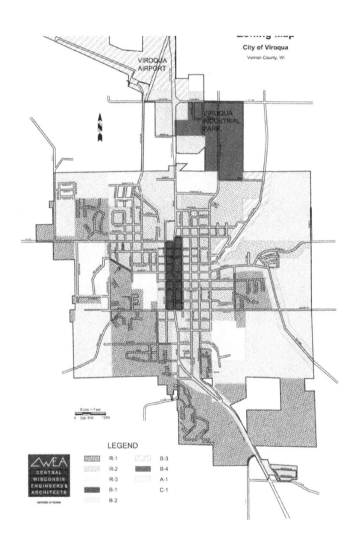

Zoning Map
City of Viroqua
Vernon County, WI

VIROQUA
AIRPORT

VIROQUA
INDUSTRIAL
PARK

Scale in Feet
0 300 600 1200

LEGEND

R-1   B-3
R-2   B-4
R-3   A-1
B-1   C-1
B-2

CWEA

CENTRAL
WISCONSIN
ENGINEERS &
ARCHITECTS

Wie komme ich vom Common Ground zum Postamt?
How do I get from the Common Ground to the post office?

Wie komme ich vom Postamt zum Kino?
How do I get from the post office to the movie theater?

Wie komme ich vom Kino zu Kristens Haus?
How do I get from the movie theater to Kristen's house?

Wie komme ich von Kristens Haus zu Itas Haus?
How do I get from Kristen's house to Ita's house?

Wie komme ich vom Landmark Center zum Friedhof?
How do I get from the Landmark Center to the cemetery?

Wie komme ich vom Supermarkt nach Kanada?
How do I get from the supermarket to Canada?

Another excellent exercise is to give the students the assignment to describe the way and give directions from their house to the school, including drawing a map preferably with some cows dotting the landscape.

Next we "go to Germany" and look at actual maps. Typically a person arrives at an airport and might have to take public transportation to their destination. Multiple exercises can be set up using street maps or maps of public transportation systems.

Exercise – directions – from Frankfurt airport – by car. You arrive at Frankfurt airport and you are renting a car. The vehicle you booked – a red BMW 328 tii – is unfortunately not available. The rental agency (named "Schrottauto") gives you instead a beat up *Trabant* ("Amisch edition") and a map of Frankfurt. Now you have to ask your way around ... answer in German, then translate into English.

(The questions would be given only in German to the students, who would need to look up the directions on the map, which has been provided to them. Then they have to write down the directions in German.)

Entschuldigung, wie komme ich nach Weilbach?
Excuse me, how do I get to Weilbach?

Entschuldigung, wie komme ich nach Flörsheim?
Excuse me, how do I get to Flörsheim?

Entschuldigung, wie komme ich nach Dreieich?
Excuse me, how do I get to Dreieich?

Entschuldigung, wie komme ich nach Ginnheim?
Excuse me, how do I get to Ginnheim?

Entschuldigung, wie komme ich nach Unterliederbach?
Excuse me, how do I get to Unterliederbach?

Entschuldigung, wie komme ich nach Bad Vilbel?
Excuse me, how do I get to Bad Vilbel?

Entschuldigung, wie komme ich nach Heusenstamm?
Excuse me, how do I get to Heusenstamm?

Entschuldigung, wie komme ich nach Königstein im Taunus?
Excuse me, how do I get to Königstein im Taunus?

Entschuldigung, wie komme ich nach Dietzenbach?
Excuse me, how do I get to Dietzenbach?

Entschuldigung, wie komme ich nach Offenbach?
Excuse me, how do I get to Offenbach?

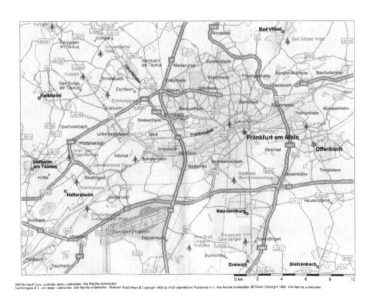

115

A somewhat more basic and simpler exercise. Here the students have to continue by themselves in that they make up follow-up questions, asking each other for directions ... and receiving the directions from their classmates ... This exercise is also suitable to be given as a homework assignment.

Excuse me, how do I get to ...
Entschuldigung, wie komme ich nach ...

Take ... until ..., then take ...
Nehmen Sie ... bis, dann nehmen Sie ...

Example/Beispiel: (You are at Frankfurt/Rhein-Main-Flughafen)

Excuse me, sweetheart, how do I get to Weilbach?
Entschuldigung, Süsse, wie komme ich nach Weilbach?

Take a left on Autobahn A3 until you get to Weilbach!
Nehmen Sie die Autobahn A3 nach links bis nach Weilbach!

In more general terms questions can be addressed as to identifying locations on the map of Germany, or give directions on how to get from one of the major cities to another. Over time the students develop a feeling for the locations and relationship to each other of the different regions of Germany.

117

Having to find your way around with public transportation is another most interesting task. Following a possible exercise using the map of the Munich "Schnellbahnnetz".

Eine Wilde Jagd Durch München.
A wild chase through Munich.

Bitte komplettieren und/oder übersetzen.
Please complte and/or translate.

You arrive at 4:30 AM at Flughafen München on Flight NCBA (NeverComeBackAirlines) #007. Your friend (Heribert) who was supposed to pick you up, overslept (as usual), and is not there, however, since he is smart (_____) he has sent you an automatically transmitted SMS to your Handy (_____) in case of his not showing up by

4:32 AM. This SMS reads: "Sorry, Mann. Nehmen Sie die S-Bahn/U-Bahn nach Kolumbusplatz und finden Sie mich in dem Kater-Karlo-Café in der Fraunhoferstraße 34"

(_____

_____

_____

_____

_____)

Give directions (in German):

Arriving at the Kater-Karlo-Café you (totally exhausted) order a triple-espresso mit Schlagsahne (_____ _____), and the dark blond waitress whispers to you in a low voice: "Heribert sagt, gehen Sie nach Petershausen!"

(_____

_____

_____

_____)

Give directions to Petershausen (in German):

Arriving in Petershausen, there is a taxi waiting for you. The taxi driver walks up to you, and says: "Halten Sie die Klappe und steigen Sie ein!

(_____

_____

_____

_____)

He drives you to Unterschleißheim where he kicks you rudely out of his beige colored perfectly clean Mercedes E320. You roll down into the dirty ditch, (_____) and hit your head (_____) on a plastic pail filled with concrete (_____). When you wake up you look up to the sky (_____) and see the following message (_____) written in a cloud (_____): "Nach Höllriegelskreuth mußt du fahren"
(_____

_____

_____)

Give directions to Höllriegelskreuth (in German):

In Höllriegelskreuth wartet Heribert am Bahnsteig. (_____). Er sagt: "Wo waren Sie so lange. Sind Sie blöd? Oder dumm? Können Sie mich nicht schneller finden?"
(_____

_____

_____

_____)

You reply: "My dear Heribert. You are ....!
(_____

_____

_____

_____

_____

_____

_____

_____)

Another very successful approach to learning about giving and following directions, which includes learning foreign languages, is the very popular "Schatzsuche", the treasure hunt. To do this we need to come up with an excellent plan, and the belief that indeed the students will be able to figure out the riddles presented to them. Once one successful treasure hunt has been established, the students (or individual students) can be asked to prepare similar treasure hunts, which they very much enjoy doing.

1. Bitte geht in das Klassenzimmer Nummer Dreihundertundfünf. Dort findet ihr eine Nachricht. Die Nachricht ist in der Nähe des Fensters versteckt. Please go into classroom number 305. There you will find a message. The message is hidden near the window.

(This is the first message, which is given to the students in a mysterious fashion. The message is printed on a piece of paper. Than the paper is cut up into small bits. Each small bit of paper contains one word. Each student receives one piece (or in a small class, several pieces). No further instructions - other than that this is a treasure hunt – are given to the students. They need to come to the realization themselves, that teamwork (!) is required, by eventually realizing that only by putting all the pieces of the puzzle together, they will be able to figure out the first clue.)

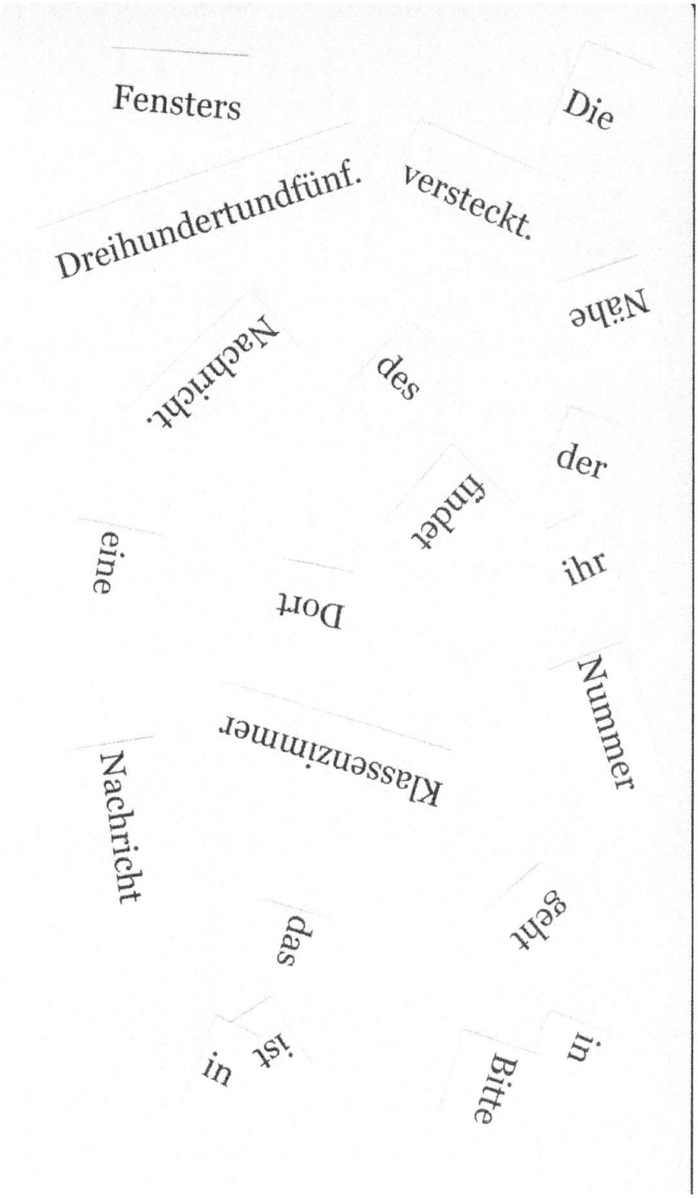

Fensters

Die

Dreihundertundfünf.

versteckt.

Nähe

Nachricht.

des

der

eine

findet

ihr

Dort

Nummer

Klassenzimmer

Nachricht

das

geht

ist

in

Bitte

in

2. Hinter dem Landmark Center ist ein Parkplatz. Der Parkplatz ist auf der Ostseite hinter dem Landmark Center. Auf dem Parkplatz steht ein Anhänger. Auf dem Anhänger befindet sich eine Nachricht.

Behind the Landmark Center (school building), there is a parking lot. The parking lot is on the east side behind the Landmark Center. In the parking lot there is a trailer. On the trailer you'll find the next message.

(This second message has been placed there – as all the following messages - beforehand.)

124

3. In der Ostallee wohnt ein Lehrer dessen zwei Söhne Schüler in unserer Schule sind. Das Haus ist weiß oder nicht? Dort findet ihr eine Nachricht in der Garage.

In the East Avenue there lives a teacher whose two sons attend our school. The house is white, or not? There you will find a message in the garage.

(The message has been hidden in this garage. It is a piece of paper, crumbled up and slightly soiled for camouflage, and stuck on a nail in the wall. The students will have to search for a while!)

4. Am Ende der Ostallee ist ein Friedhof. Dort findet ihr die nächste Nachricht in dem Mülleimer.

At the end of East Avenue, there is a cemetery. There you will find the next message in a waste container.

(Indeed - after a 5 minute hike to the cemetery, the students discover a note in a garbage bin.)

5. Zwei amerikanische Präsidenten müßt ihr kennen. Dann findet ihr die Kreuzung von zwei Straßen benannt nach den zwei Präsidenten. An dieser

Kreuzung steht eine Kirche. Die Kirche ist groß und weiß. Dort findet ihr eine Nachricht in der Regenrinne.

You need to know two American presidents. Then you will find the crossroads of two streets named after the two presidents. At this crossroads there is a church. The church is large and white. There you will find a message in a gutter.

(Again – after some time spent searching, the students discover a note hidden in a rain spout. Hopefully they did not climb up the side of the building to check the rain gutters at the church tower!)

6. Geht in das Landmark Center. Da gibt es ein Schulbüro. In dem Büro ist eine schwarze (oder nicht schwarz?) Schublade wo die Erste Hilfe Sachen sind. In der Schublade ist eine Nachricht.

Now go back to the Landmark Center. There is an office. In the office, there is a black (or not black?) drawer, with the First Aid supplies. In the drawer there is a message.

(And there is!)

7. Geht zurück zu dem Klassenzimmer Nummer Dreihundertundzwei. Dort steht ein Schreibtisch. Der Schatz ist in dem Schreibtisch oder vielleicht in dem Schrank.

Now go back to classroom number 302. There is a desk. The treasure is inside the desk or perhaps in the closet.

(Now the student will find the treasure: German chocolate of course! The students will divide it among themselves.)

Germans Are Funny

Chapter 7: *Bildergeschichten und Filme (Stories with Pictures and Movies)*

Make your own picture book. When on vacation, take a few photos, and add some story to it. Then turn this into a presentation, showing the photos and telling the story. Or make it into a power point presentation using a video projector. Ask the students to come up with their own creations. I am extremely proud of having inspired my students to create short movies (in German). But watch out. This can be contagious, and soon the students will make movies for other classes too. Please watch the famous student created short movie "Das Chip". It can be found on www.yihs.net/gallery; if you like James Bond movies, you'll love this one!

Following, please find a power point type presentation of a Dadaistic photo story.

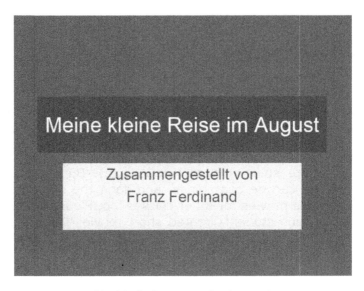

My Little Journey in August
Put together by Franz Ferdinand

Ein
Baum
und ein
großer
Stein

A tree and a large boulder

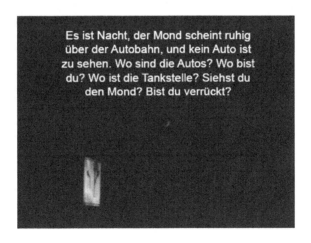

It is night, the moon shines quietly above the interstate, and not a car is in sight. Where are the cars? Where are you? Where is the gas station? Do you see the moon? Are you crazy?

Ah – a blue flag. How beautiful!

Finally a cup of coffee. The background is black and the ground is yellow. Strange.

Links abbiegen verboten. Wie geht es nun weiter? Ich muß jetzt doch nach links ...

Left turn not allowed. How do I go on? I really have to go left ...

Ja – jetzt eine Pause. So ein schöner Stuhl; und daneben ein paar Geschenke. Dann verschwinde ich durch die Türe ...

Yes – now a break. Such a beautiful chair; and next to it some presents. Then I disappear through the door ...

Auf der anderen Seite: ein Sandhaufen. Wo ist meine kleine rote Schaufel und mein gelber Kübel?

On the other side: A pile of sand. Where is my little red shovel and my yellow bucket?

Ich versuche Äpfel zu Essen. Aber die Äpfel sind schrecklich sauer. Pfui!

I try to eat apples. But the apples are awfully sour. Bah.

Finally I find a friend: A yellow hydrant. He laughs and rattles his chains.

In the afternoon I arrive in Greece. Here you see the Parthenon on the Acropolis.

Two friendly monks greet me: "Welcome in Athens"
Please park your car behind the mountain."

The harbor of Piraeus. Where are the ships? It is
Saturday in the afternoon; ships are there only
Monday through Friday.

Der Fels von Piräus. Dort saß einst
Aphrodite und kämmte ihr langes Haar.

The rock of Piraeus. Aphrodite sat there once and combed her long hair.

Sparta – hier kommt niemand rein

Sparta – no one enters here!

The night is dark. I travel via speed boat from Greece to ...

5:30 AM – I arrive in Canada!!!

Kanada hat endlose Weizenfelder. Sonst nichts.

In Canada you see endless wheat fields. Nothing else.

Mit einen Kanu navigiere ich den Sankt Laurenz Seeweg. Es ist kalt, aber ...

I navigate in a canoe through the St. Lawrence sea way. It is cold, but ...

my canoe has GPS and a turbo paddle. Within 15 minutes I race past Montreal.

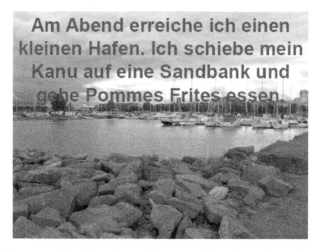

In the evening I arrive at a small harbor. I push my canoe onto a sandbar and go to eat fries.

Nach einem langen Tag auf dem Wasser, ist der Seemann glücklich, wenn der Wasserhahn funktioniert.
(Sir Admiral Nelson)

After a long day on the water, the seaman is happy, if the water faucet functions. (Sir Admiral Nelson)

Germans Are Funny

Chapter 8: *Die Übersetzung (Translations)*

Translation exercises need to be given to the students like a steady diet of healthy foods. Translation exercises can be presented in a variety of ways. The handwritten note – as long as it is legible – is just as educational as the beautiful printed page including illustrations and pictures. Modern technology has given us additional devices that we can use. A video projector provides the possibility to work with electronic media also in this realm. A text or image projected on the wall creates a different focus for the class as compared to individual worksheets, and can be used pedagogically with great success. Following you find a variety of translation exercises for different skill levels. These exercises are usually given to the students to work on individually or to be worked on in small groups. The use of dictionaries is permitted – finding words in the dictionary is an important skill to learn.

Die Bärenhöhle.

Unterhalb der Stadt Viroqua gibt es eine große Höhle. In der Höhle wohnen viele Bären. Die Bären essen Honig und Blaubeeren. Zwei der Bären heissen Johnny und Susi. Am Samstag gehen Johnny und Susi zu dem Supermarkt. Sie müssen Honig und Blaubeeren kaufen. Johnny kauft 5 Pfund Honig, und Susi kauft 7 Pfund Blaubeeren. Susi und Johnny haben ein Moped. Sie fahren mit dem Moped auf der Chicago Allee bis zu der Polizeistation. Hinter der Polizeistation verstecken sie das Moped. Die Höhle der Bären ist dort in der Nähe. Die Bären haben sogar einen Briefkasten. Auf dem Briefkasten kannst du lesen: "Bärenhöhle. Betreten verboten!"

The Bears' Cave.

Underneath the city of Viroqua there is a huge cave. In the cave live many bears. The bears eat honey and blueberries. Two of the bears are named Johnny and Susi. On Saturday Johnny and Susi go to the supermarket. They need to buy honey and blueberries. Johnny buys 5 pounds of honey, and Susi buys 7 pounds of blueberries. Susi and Johnny own a moped. They ride the moped on Chicago Avenue up to the police station. They hide the moped behind the police station. The bears' cave is near there. The bears even have a mail box. You can read what's written on the mail box: "Bears' cave. No admittance!"

This or similar exercises can also be used in a multi-level classroom, giving students of the different levels individualized instructions, for example:

Level 1: Underline the nouns (hint: nouns are capitalized) – look up the nouns in the dictionary and write them underneath the German nouns

Level 2: Complete level 1. Translate the text roughly into English.

Level 3 and 4: Translate the text into English. Underline all verbs. Conjugate the verbs on the back of this paper.
Übersetze und beantworte die Fragen.

Susi Sorglos fliegt von Richland Center nach Hamburg mit einem Airbus 330. Was ist ein Airbus?

In Hamburg, Susi kauft ein Moped und fährt nach Dänemark. Wie heißt die Hauptstadt von Dänemark?

Susi fährt neunhundertsiebenundachtzig Kilometer mit dem Moped. Dann ist das Moped kaputt! Warum?

Susi nimmt ein Schiff und landet in Schweden. Über welches Meer fährt sie? Nordsee oder Ostsee?

Susi sagt: "Ah, wie schön ist es in Skandinavien. Der Schnee ist himmlisch weiß, der Wind ist kühl, die Bäume sind so supergrün, der Kaffee ist dunkelschwarz, und mein neuer Volvo ist einfach wahnsinnig gut. Wohin fährt Susi mit dem Volvo?

Welche Länder sind in Skandinavien?
1.
2.
3.

Plötzlich denkt Susi: "Ach, ich möchte in den Süden reisen! Nach Griechenland oder die Türkei." Zehn Minuten später fliegt Susi mit einer Boeing 777 nach Ankara. Wo ist Ankara?

Susi fährt mit dem Zug von Ankara nach Westen. Welches Land besucht sie?

Susi mietet einen VW Golf IV und fährt nach Bukarest. Wo ist Bukarest und wieviel kostet das Benzin in Bukarest?

Susi ist müde. Was macht sie jetzt?

Translate and answer the questions.

Susi Carefree flies from Richland Center to Hamburg in an Airbus 330. What is an Airbus?

Susi buys a moped in Hamburg and rides to Denmark. What is the name of the capital of Denmark?

Susi travels nine hundred eighty seven kilometers on the moped. Now the moped is broken! Why?

Susi takes a ship and lands in Sweden. She traveled on which ocean? North Sea or Baltic Sea?

Susi says: "Ah, how beautiful it is in Scandinavia. The snow is heavenly white, the wind cool, the trees are so super green, the coffee so dark black, and my new Volvo is simply crazy-like great. Where will Susi travel with the new Volvo?

Which countries are there in Scandinavia?
1.
2.
3.

Suddenly Susi thinks: "Well, I want to travel to the South! To Greece or Turkey." Ten minutes later Susi is flying in a Boeing 777 to Ankara. Where is Ankara?

Susi travels via train from Ankara westwards. Which land is she going to visit?

Susi rents a VW Golf IV and drives to Bucarest. Where is Bucarest and how much do you pay for gas in Bucarest?

Susi is tired. What does she do now?

Heribert Hintermeyer.

Heribert Hintermeyer wohnt in der Amalienstraße 1356 b. Heribert fährt mit einem grünen *Mercedes SLK 3.2 Liter Turbo* von München nach *Berlin über die Autobahn. Was ist die Geschwindigkeitsbegrenzung? Antwort:*

Plötzlich ist der *Mercedes* kaputt. Der Auspuff fällt weg. Heribert muß zu Fuß gehen. Er geht zweiundzwanzig Kilometer bis er nach einer Stadt kommt. Wie heißt die Stadt? Antwort:

Heribert geht zu dem Supermarkt namens "der Schweinestall". Was kauft er? Antwort:

Dann möchte Heribert zu dem Restaurant *Grünstein* fahren. Wie macht er das? Antwort:

Was bestellt Heribert im Restaurant *Grünstein*? Antwort:

Heribert nimmt die Gabel und das Messer und ißt ...., dann trinkt er ....

Um 19 Uhr 33 rennt Heribert aus dem Restaurant. Warum? Antwort:

Die Polizei kommt und verhaftet Heribert um 20 Uhr 34 als er seine Schuhe in den Fluß wirft. Warum? Antwort:

Heribert Hintermeyer.

Heribert Hintermeyer lives in the Amalien Street 1356 b. Heribert drives in a green Mercedes SLK 3.2 turbo from Munich to Berlin via the Interstate. What is the speed limit? Answer:

Suddenly the Mercedes breaks down. The muffler falls off. Heribert needs to go on foot. He walks twenty two kilometers until he reaches a city. What is the name of the city? Answer:

Heribert walks to the supermarket named "pig sty". What does he buy? Answer:

Now Heribert wants to drive to the restaurant *Grünstein*. How does he do that? Answer:

What does Heribert order at the Restaurant *Grünstein*? Answer:

Heribert takes the fork and the knife and eats ………………., then he drinks ………………..

At 7:33 PM Heribert dashes out of the restaurant. Why? Answer:

The police arrives and arrests Heribert at 8:34 PM while he is throwing his shoes into the river. Why? Answer:

Bei Susi.

Am Samstag geht (gehen) Heribert zu Susi nach München. Heribert nimmt (nehmen) die S-Bahn von Rosenheim nach München-Hauptbahnhof. Dann fährt (fahren) er mit der U-Bahn nach München-Nord. Susi wohnt (wohnen) in der Leopoldstraße 356 ½ B. Susi ist (sein) Vegetarierin. Sie kocht (kochen) Sojaburger und Grünkern für den lieben Heribert. Heribert lacht (lachen) und trinkt (trinken) eine Limonade. Dann gehen Susi und Heribert mit dem Hund namens "Schnauzerl" spazieren. Plötzlich rennt (rennen) Schnauzerl in das McDonald's Restaurant. Schnauzerl frißt (fressen) eine Mahlzeit #2 mit zwei Käsehamburgers und superviel Pommes Frites mit wenig Ketschup. Heribert kauft (kaufen) ein Eis mit Sahne ohne Ketschup. Susi wartet (warten) draußen. Dann laufen (laufen) alle drei zurück zu Susis Wohnung.

At Susi's.

On Saturday Heribert goes (to go) to Susi in Munich. Heribert takes (to take) the train from Rosenheim to Munich's main train station. Then he travels (to travel) via the subway to North Munich. Susi lives (to live) in the Leopold Street 356 ½ B. Susi is (to be) a vegetarian. She cooks (to cook) soy burgers and Grünkern for the lovely Heribert. Heribert laughs (to laugh) and drinks (to drink) a lemonade. Then Susi and Heribert go on a walk with the dog named "Schnauzerl". Suddenly Schnauzerl races (to race) into the McDonald's restaurant. Schnauzerl eats (to eat) a meal #2 including two cheeseburgers and lots of fries with little ketchup. Heribert buys (to buy) icecream with whipping cream without ketchup. Susi waits (to wait) outside. Then all three jog (to jog) back to Susi's place.

Level 1: Underline the nouns (hint: nouns are capitalized) – look up the nouns in the dictionary and write them underneath the German nouns

Level 2: Complete level 1. Translate the text roughly into English.

Level 3 and 4: Translate the text into English. Underline all verbs. Conjugate the verbs on the back of this paper.

Level 5: Go to the Common Ground Café and bring back Kaffee und Kuchen (coffee and cake) for everyone.

Often it is helpful to give some vocabulary or some verbs in the infinite form. These can either be put into the text, or written down on the blackboard for the students to see, when they look up in despair after working for a while at the translation exercise. The following translation exercise has also the purpose to learn adjectives. Students should be asked to underline the adjectives. An additional task could be to ask the students to replace all adjectives with other ones, thereby changing the story in an interesting manner. The new creations can then be shared by asking some of the students to recite their creations.

Im Blauen Wald.
Am Mittwoch geht der liebe Herr Meier in den blauen Wald. Der kleine Herr Meier hat eine kleine, schwache Motorsäge. Er will einen riesengroßen Baum fällen (to cut down). Der böse Baum sagt: "Paß auf, du kleiner Mensch! Ich falle (to fall) auf deinen kleinen Kopf." Herr Meier nimmt (to take) die gelbe Motosäge und schneidet (to cut) den lieben Baum. Der rosarote Baum fällt auf den kleinen Zeh des Herrn Meier. "Autsch, autsch, autsch, autsch, autsch, autsch @#%&^$!," schreit (to shout) Herr Meier. Herr Meiers Zeh ist unter dem gelben Baum. Das tut (to do) weh! Herr Meier nimmt sein schlechtes Handy (cell phone), und telephoniert die Polizei. Die Polizei kommt zu Herr Meier, und sagt: "Ach, du netter Herr Meier, warum ist dein Zeh unter dem gelben Baum?" Herr Meier ist schon blau im Gesicht, und stöhnt (to sigh): "Ich weiß nicht!"

In the Blue Forest.
On Wednesday the lovely Mr. Meier goes into the blue forest. The little Mr. Meier has a small, weak chain saw. He wants to cut down a gigantic tree. The evil tree says: "Watch out, you little man! I will

fall onto your little head." Mr. Meier takes the yellow chain saw and cuts the lovely tree. The pink tree falls on Mr. Meier's little toe. "Ouch, ouch, ouch, ouch, ouch, ouch @#%&^$!," shouts Mr. Meier. Mr. Meier's toe is under the yellow tree. That does hurt! Mr. Meier takes his inferior cell phone, and calls the police. The policeman comes to where Mr. Meier is, and says: "Well, my nice Mr. Meier, why is your toe underneath the yellow tree?" Mr. Meier is already blue in the face, and sighs: "I don't know!"

Sport ist Mord.

Am Montag, spiele ich Fußball. Ich falle auf meine Nase. Am Dienstag, reite ich mein Pferd. Das Pferd wirft mich in den Graben. Am Mittwoch, gehe ich Snowboarden. Ich lande im tiefen Schnee. Das tut weh. Am Donnerstag, spiele ich Tennis. Ein Ball trifft mich auf dem linken Ohr. Am Freitag, gehe ich zum Boxen. Ich boxe meinen Freund auf das Kinn. Mein Freund ist nicht mehr mein Freund. Am Samstag, gehe ich zum Rennfahren. Die Polizei verhaftet mich. Am Sonntag, spiele ich American Football. Ich breche meinen rechten kleinen Zeh. Mein Bruder sagt: "Sport ist Mord!"

Sport is Murder.

On Monday I play soccer. I fall on my nose. On Tuesday I ride my horse. The horse throws me in the ditch. On Wednesday I go snowboarding. I land in a snowdrift. That hurts. On Thursday I play tennis. A ball hits my left ear. On Friday I go boxing. I box my friend's chin. My friend is no longer my friend. On Saturday I go racing. The police arrests me. On Sunday I play football. I break my right little toe. My brother says: "Sport is murder!"

Geschwindigkeitsbegrenzung.

Außenminister F. fährt mit einem Volvo C40 von Berlin über Nürnberg nach München. Er besucht Ministerpräsident S. in S.'s Haus in der Amalienstraße. F. trinkt eine Cola, und ißt Oliven. S. trinkt dunkeles Starkbier, und ißt Sojakäse. Die beiden Politiker verhandeln einen Beschluß. Oder ist es vielleicht eine Verschwörung? F. will eine Geschwindigkeitsbeschränkung von 120 km/h für die Autobahn autorisieren. S. denkt: "Das ist Verrat. Wir werden einen Krawall haben. Oder vielleicht eine Revolution." S. sagt: "Ich muß das zurückweisen." F. fragt: "Vielleicht möchtest du mehr Starkbier?" Da schreit S.: "Ohne mich. Ich fahre mit meinem BMW immer 240 km/h!" F. antwortet: "Du bist ein Tyrann. Du trinkst zuviel Starkbier. Und du bist uncool!"

Speed Limit.

Secretary of State F. drives with a Volvo C40 from Berlin via Nuremberg to Munich. He visits Prime Minister S. in S.'s house in the Amalien Street. F. drinks a cola, and eats olives. S. drinks dark strong beer, and eats soy cheese. Both politicians negotiate a treaty. Or perhaps it is a conspiracy? F. wants to authorize a speed limit of 120 km/h for the Interstate. S. thinks: "This is treason. We will have a riot. Or maybe a revolution." S. says: "I have to reject this." F. asks: "Perhaps you would like more strong beer?" Now S. yells: "Without me. I always drive with my BMW at 240 km/h!" F. answers: "You are a tyrant. You drink to much strong beer. And you are not cool!"

Bitte übersetzen und beantworten.
Please translate and answer.

Wo bin ich heute nicht?
Where am I not today?

Wo bitte ist die Autobahn?
Where please is the Interstate?

Welche Farbe hat die U-Bahn?
What color is the subway?

Wo bitte ist der Schnee?
Where please is the snow?

Wo oh wo ist das Taxi?
Where oh where is the Taxi?

Wo ist das rote Mietauto?
Where is the red rental car?

Wo ist ein vegetarisches Restaurant?
Where is a vegetarian Restaurant?

Hast du einen Geldautomat in deinem Badezimmer?
Do you have an ATM in your bathroom?

Kann ich mit der Kreditkarte Kanu fahren?
Can I go canoeing with the credit card?

Wieviel kostet eine halbe Banane?
How much is half a banana?

Wo bitte ist die Damentoilette (Herrentoilette)?
Where please is the women's room (men's room)?

Wo sind meine rotweißblauen Schuhe?
Where are my red, white, and blue shoes?

Wieviel Uhr ist es um 12 Uhr?
What time is it at 12 o'clock?

Wo ist mein gelbes Handy?
Where is my yellow cell phone?

Wo ist ein kleiner Supermarkt?
Where is a little supermarket?

Wo ist eine schlechte Bäckerei?
Where is a lousy bakery?

Wo ist die tote, schwarzweiße Kuh?
Where is the dead, black and white cow?

Wo sind die Polizisten heute?
Where are the policemen today?

Wo ist mein kleiner Mercedes?
Where is my little Mercedes?

Wo ist das schöne Gefängnis?
Where is the beautiful jailhouse?

Wo ist das leise Punkrockkonzert?
Where is the quiet punk rock concert?

Wo ist die langweilige Disko?
Where is the boring disco?

Wo ist mein Papa?
Where is my dad?

Following another mixed exercise. Level 1 students have smaller, easier tasks to fulfill, than the more advanced students. It is very common, especially in smaller schools, that a foreign language class has mixed levels, and it is helpful to find ways of always coming up with exercises that are challenging and appropriate for the different levels.

Übersetzung vom Englischen ins Deutsche
Translation from English into German

Level 1/2/3 – translate: Germany is a federal republic with 14 federal states.

Level 2/3 – answer: The 14 federal states are:

Level 1/2/3 – translate: The German emperor is called Gerhard Schröder. (True or false?)

Level 1/2/3 – translate: The German foreign secretary, Joschka Fischer, is a rioter. (True or false?)

Level 1/2/3 – translate: Politicians from all parties like to party. Do you know any German parties?

Level 2/3 – answer: The German parties are:

Level 1/2/3 – translate: Schröder says: "Vote for me, my legislation is no conspiracy, or do you want the state of emergency? See - I am a poet like Goethe!"

Level 1/2/3 – translate: Foreign secretary Fischer flies to Chicago to see the movie Chicago. His comment: "Overwhelming!"

Level 1/2/3 – translate: A lonely member of parliament is an opponent to the supporters of the cabinet, but loves the program.

Level 1/2/3 – translate: We reject democracy, we demonstrate for the monarchy, we riot at every session, we negotiate nothing, we authorize no legislation, we don't vote, we are ...

Level 2/3 – answer:

Here is a more simple exercise concerning picture-word-connections. (See pictures next page).

Level 1 and 2: Identify 12 items and write them down in English and German.

Level 3 and 4: Identify all items and write them down in English and German; write sentences concerning the items.

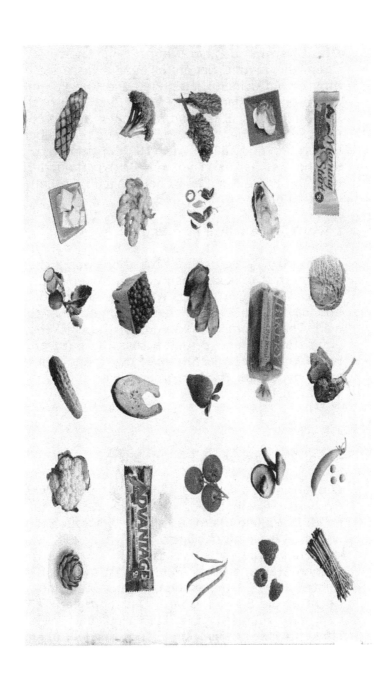

Level 1 – übersetze ins Englische

Die Chemie. Es war einmal ein Chemiker. Der Chemiker nimmt Sauerstoff und Wasserstoff und mixt es auf seinem Bauernhof. Die Kuh kommt aus dem Stall und sagt: "Muh!" Der Chemiker riecht die Schwefelsäure. Das sind die alten Eier von den Hühnern. Die Eier stinken. Eine Maus rennt über den Bauernhof und fällt in das H2O in dem Klo. Mein Freund Piet hat viel Dynamit. Er experimentiert mit dem Dynamit. Der Bauernhof fliegt in die Luft. Das ist schade.

Level 1 – translate into English

Chemistry. Once upon a time there was a chemist. The chemist takes oxygen and hydrogen and mixes them at his farm. The cow comes out of the barn and says: "Moo!" The chemist smells the sulfuric acid. That's from the old eggs of the chickens. The eggs stink. A mouse runs across the barnyard and falls into the H2O in the toilet. My friend Piet has a lot of dynamite. He experiments with the dynamite. The farmstead explodes. Pity.

Level 2 – übersetze ins Englische

Die Chemie. Es war einmal ein Chemiker namens Gerhard. Er wohnt in der Nähe von Westby auf dem Land. Der blöde Chemiker nimmt viel Sauerstoff und wenig Wasserstoff und mixt es auf seinem Bauernhof. Die scharz-weisse Kuh kommt aus dem grünen Stall und sagt: "Muh! Wo ist mein Futter, du Idiot?" Der Chemiker denkt sehr viel und dann riecht er die Schwefelsäure. Das sind die alten Eier von den Hühnern. Die Eier sind blau-grün und stinken. Eine Maus rennt superschnell über den Bauernhof und fällt plötzlich in das H2O in dem kleinen Klo. Mein Freund Piet hat viel zu viel

Dynamit. Er experimentiert ein bisschen mit dem Dynamit. Der Bauernhof fliegt in die Luft. Bummmmmmmmm! Das ist vielleicht schade.

Level 2 – translate into English

Chemistry. Once upon a time there was a chemist named Gerhard. He lives near Westby in the country. The stupid chemist takes lots of oxygen and little hydrogen and mixes them at his farm. The black and white cow comes out of the green barn and says: "Moo! Where is my fodder, you idiot?" The chemist thinks a lot and then he smells the sulfuric acid. That's from the old eggs of the chickens. The eggs are blue-green and stink. A mouse runs very fast across the barnyard and falls suddenly into the H2O in the little toilet. My friend Piet has way to much dynamite. He experiments a little with the dynamite. The farmstead explodes. Booooooooooom! Perhaps a pity.

Level 3 – übersetze ins Englische

Die Chemie. Es waren einmal zwei Chemiker namens Gerhard und Werner. Sie wohnen in der Nähe von dir auf dem Land. Die blöden Idioten-Chemiker suchen viel Sauerstoff und wenig Wasserstoff auf einem Bauernhof. Die gelben Schafe kommen aus dem winzigen Stall und sagen: "Bääääh! Wo ist meine Zeitung, du Blödkopf?" Der Chemist liest sehr viel, aber er kann die Schwefelsäure nicht riechen. Das sind nicht die alten Eier von den Hühnern. Die Eier sind keineswegs blau-grün und stinken nicht. Eine Maus joggt sehr langsam über den Bauernhof und fällt ganz langsam in das H2O in dem grossen Klo. Mein Freund Piet hat leider Dynamit. Er schmeisst das Dynamit in das grosse Klo. Das Klo fliegt nicht in die Luft. Hmmmmmmmmmm! Das ist vielleicht nicht schade.

Level 3 – translate into English

Chemistry. Once upon a time there were two chemists named Gerhard and Werner. They live near you in the country. The stupid idiot-chemists search for lots of oxygen and little hydrogen at a farm. The yellow sheep come out of the tiny barn and say: "Bah! Where is my newspaper, you blockhead?" The chemist reads very much, but he cannot smell the sulfuric acid. That are not the old eggs of the chickens. The eggs are certainly not blue-green and do not stink. A mouse jogs very slowly across the barnyard and falls very slowly into the H2O in the huge toilet. My friend Piet unfortunately has dynamite. He throws the dynamite into the huge toilet. The toilet does not explode. Hmmm! That is perhaps not a pity.

Level 4 – translate into German

The Chemistry. I go to the Chemist and buy dynamite. The Chemist says: "Sorry, pal. Your credit card is not good." Then I go to the Westby police station and ask for dynamite. The female police officer says: "Sorry, dude. You look too young to have that." Well, then I drive with my snowmobile over the fields to a nice little farm south of Westby. I go into the hay loft and look for old stinky eggs. I collect 209 horribly smelling eggs. I mix the eggs with equal parts carbon dioxide and shoe shine and light the fuse. Nothing happens.

Warnung.

In den Trümmern der Roburitfabrik lagert noch eine große Menge von Stoffen, die nach Ansicht Sachverständiger jeden Augenblick zur Explosion gelangen kann. Es wird deßhalb gewarnt, sich der Unglücksstelle zu nähern.

Witten, 29. November 1906.

Der Oberbürgermeister:

Dr. Haarmann.

Germans Are Funny

Chapter 9: *Der Test (Tests)*

Tests can be fun too. I believe in frequent testing as a means to gauge students' progress (or lack thereof) both for the teacher and educator, but also for the students themselves, as they embark on their journey into adulthood. Naturally it is important to keep in mind that tests always concern themselves with certain skills, while neglecting others, so much so that a wise head (!) came up with the definition: "The intelligence test measures the intelligence that the intelligence test measures." However, it is possible to bring a certain amount of artistry into each test, so that students feel connected to the process of taking the test in a different way, and regard the results of their efforts in a somewhat more positive light compared to a purely intellectual exercise. On the following pages you will find some examples. I usually create the tests in such a way that they are increasingly difficult, so that the beginners in a course can deal with questions they are able to answer at the beginning of the test pages, while the advanced students quickly advance to the later pages in the test, and have to turn therefore to more difficult tasks. It is a good idea to have an open ended task as the last task of the test – for instance, to create a story, short play, dialogue, etc. – so that really advanced students, who quickly move through the rest of the test, still have some work to do, even after they have completed the rest of the test.

Test (Thema: "Wetter")
Test (Theme: "Weather")

Name:
Name:

Datum:
Date:

1. Describe today's weather in Railroad Flats, Wisconsin by creating a fictional weather report (in German)

2. Describe today's weather in Rosenheim (Germany) by creating a fictional weather report (in German)

3. Create a poem using weather vocabulary

4. **Übersetze:** Ich hasse die Hitzewelle im Januar. Ich liebe den Schneesturm im Kuhstall. Die Schneeflocke und der Orkan und der Wirbelwind und der Donnerschlag und der Nießelregen und der Regenbogen und die Wolke tanzen den Tango. Heribert sagt: "Schau, schau, liebe Susi, das Thermometer ist kaputt. Der Schnee fällt auf Herr Frosty Schneemann und Frau Schnorkelson macht Donner." Der Nebel hängt in Westby, aber in Liberty Pole scheint die Sonne! Der Luftdruck ist nicht schön, es ist stürmisch, kalt, neblig, frostig, bedeckt, und dunstig. Das Klima in Viroqua ist nicht warm wie in den Tropen. Der Kommissar kommt und schreit: "Schlecht! Klar!! Dunkel!!! Trocken!!!! Frisch!!!!! Naß? Frostig?? Schwül??!

Translate: I hate the heat wave in January. I love the snow storm in the barn. The snow flake and the hurricane and the tornado and the thunder clap and the drizzle and the rainbow and the cloud dance the tango. Heribert says: "Look, look, dear Susi, the thermometer is broken. The snow falls on Mr. Frosty Snowman and Mrs. Schnorkelson makes thunder." The fog hangs in Westby, but in Liberty Pole the sun shines! The barometric pressure is not beautiful, it is stormy, cold, foggy, frosty, cloudy, and hazy. The climate in Viroqua is not warm like in the tropics. The inspector arrives and shouts: "Bad! Clear!! Dark!!! Dry!!!! Fresh!!!!! Wet? Frosty?? Muggy??!

5. Konjugiere the folgenden Verben.
Conjugate the following verbs.

blasen (to blow)
wechseln (to change)
fallen (to fall)
schmelzen (to melt)
regnen (to rain)
wärmen (to warm)
pfeifen (to whistle)

6. Beschreibe auf Deutsch.
Describe in German.

7. Beschreibe auf Deutsch.
Describe in German.

8. Vervollständige die Geschichte unter Nummer 4.
Complete the story found at number 4.

Next please find a short quiz that relates again to the word sense. The students are presented with vocabulary words, which they had learned in previous sessions, all relating to food, restaurant and cooking. The words are given in a misspelled fashion, and the students are meant to correct them. *(Correct spelling and translation in italics).*

Superkleines Quizlein
Very little tiny quiz

Name:
Name:

Datum:
Date:

Korrigiere die Rechtschreibung und übersetze.
Correct the spelling and translate.

das Wirtshouse
das Wirtshaus
tavern

der Kafee
der Kaffee
coffee

die Speißekartze
die Speisekarte
menu

der Nachtish
der Nachtisch
dessert

das Schwienefliesch
das Scheinefleisch
pork

der Barten
der Braten
roast

die Würst
die Wurst
sausage

das Hühnafleusch
das Hühnerfleisch
chicken

das Gewürs
das Gewürz
spice

das Rührbrei
das Rührei
scrambled eggs

das Stiegelwei
das Spiegelei
fried egg (sunny side up)

die Gedreiteflokcen
die Getreideflocken
grain flakes

der Katoffelbei
der Kartoffelbrei
mashed potatoes

die Chokolate
die Schokolade
chocolate

The next test related to a previous session, when a newspaper report about a collision of a ferry boat and a sightseeing steamer, has been studied.

Zwei Verletzte nach Schiffskollision.

Großeinsatz im Hamburger Hafen: Ein Ausflugsdampfer mit 91 Passagieren an Bord und ein Fährschiff sind am Nachmittag zusammen gestoßen. Zwei Löschboote und sechs Rettungswagen wurden zum Unfallort beordert. Zwei Passagiere mussten ins Krankenhaus gebracht werden. Die Einsatzkräfte waren zunächst von mehreren Verletzten ausgegangen und hatten einen Großalarm ausgelöst. Warum das Fährschiff und der Ausflugsdampfer gegen 15 Uhr kollidiert waren, war noch unklar. Menschliches Versagen wird nicht ausgeschlossen, sagte Feuerwehr-Sprecher Schneider.

der Verletzte	injured (person)
der Großeinsatz	huge emergency
der Ausflugsdampfer	sightseeing steamboat
das Fährschiff	ferry
sind zusammen gestoßen	have collided
das Löschboot	amphibious fire brigade
der Rettungswagen	ambulance
wurden beordert	were dispatched
mussten gebracht werden	had to be transported
die Einsatzkräfte	emergency personnel
waren ausgegangen	had assumed
hatten ausgelöst	(had) caused
unklar	unclear
das Versagen	error
wird nicht ausgeschlossen	has not been ruled out

Now the students are presented with the following test relating to the newspaper article studied in the previous session.

Test
Test

Name:
Name (yours):

1. Which headline is correct?
A. Zwei Verletzte nach Schiffskollision
B. Verletzte, zwei nach Schiffskollision
C. Nach Schiffskollision zwei Verletzte
D. Nach Verletze zwei Schiffskollision

2. Which sentence is correct?
A. 91 Passagieren an Bord und ein Fährschiff sind am Nachmittag zusammen gestoßen mit einem Ausflugsdampfer.
B. Ein Ausflugsdampfer mit 91 Passagieren an Bord und ein Fährschiff sind am Nachmittag zusammen gestoßen.
C. Ein Ausflugsdampfer und ein Fährschiff sind mit 91 Passagieren am Nachmittag zusammen gestoßen an Bord.
D. Ein Ausflugsdampfer am Nachmittag mit 91 Passagieren an Bord und ein Fährschiff sind zusammen gestoßen.

3. Which one is correct? Circle one correct one per line.
A. Zwei/zwie
B. Passagieres/Passageire/passagiere/Passagiere
C. müssten/mussten/mußten/müßten
D. ins/bins/kins/schins
E. Krankenhuus/Kränkenhaus/Krankenhaus/Kronk-haus/Crankyhouse
F. gebraucht/gebrächt/gebracht/gebrachtet/gebrach
G. werdin/werden/worden/schnorden.

4. Fill in the right one.
A. Feuerwehr-Sprecher Schneider ....
...................(sagte/klagte/meinte/schweinte/weinte)

B. Das Fährschiff und der Ausflugsdampfer ....….…... (sagten/kollidierten/collided /essen/saufen)

C. Zwei Verletzte sind ....
....................….... (verschissen, verletzt, versauft, verschönt, kollidiert)

D. Die Feuerwehr hat ein ....……. (Ampel, Fährschiff, Löschboot, kaltes Sandwich mit Hering)

Another short test relating to one of the dictations (see chapter 1).

Test
Test

Name:
Name (yours):

Translate into German
murder
movie
movie theater
cash register
song
adventure
field
poisoned
murderer

Translate into English
der Motorschlitten
die Kartoffelchips
die Wurst mit Senf
die Winterjacke
die Kartoffelchipabteilung
die Hauptrolle
das Röcheln
das Handy

Translate: Heribert geht mit Susi und Franz-Heinrich zum Wal-Mart und kauft fünfzig Fantas, zweihundertdreiunddreizig Kartoffelchips, eine Winterjacke, vierundachtzig Würste mit viel Senf, sechstausendachthundertzwölf Liter Schnaps und ein neues, grünes Handy.

Heribert goes with Susi and Franz-Heinrich to Wal-Mart and buys 50 Fantas, 263 potato chips, 1 winter jacket, 84 sausages with lots of mustard, 6812 liter schnapps and a new, green mobile phone.

advanced levels
Re-create the story (of Franz-Heinrich's unexpected death) from memory and write it down in German

Two movies that are highly recommended by me to be shown to the students, which will help them immensely to understand the recent German history and culture, are "Die Verlorene Ehre der Katharina Blum", and "Goodbye, Lenin!" Katharina Blum is based on the novel of the same title by Nobel laureate Heinrich Böll, who in this scathing portrayal of the boulevard press and their influence on people and society, paints a realistic, if somewhat depressing picture of West German society in the 1970s. "Goodbye, Lenin!" is a humorous look at the events surrounding the fall of the Berlin Wall in 1989. Both movies are available in the USA (at netflix.com) in German original with English subtitles, which – depending on the level of language skills among the students – you might decide to turn on or off. Following you will find two tests that relate to the two movies.

Kommissar Beizmenne (Mario Adorf, links) verhört die festgenommene Katharina Blum (Angela Winkler, 2.v.links).

Test
Test

Ich heiße _____
My name is _____

Heute ist _____
Today is _____

Translate and/or answer or comment –

1. "Dieser Ring ist acht bis zehntausend Mark wert"
"This ring is worth eight to ten thousand marks"

2. How did Ludwig Götten escape from Katharina's apartment?

3. "Sie haben eine Eigentumswohnung? Wieviel kostet das?" fragt Kommissar Beizmenne.
"You own an apartment? How much do you pay for that?" Inspector Beizmenne asks.

4. In was für einem Haus lebt Katharina?
In what kind of building does Katharian live?

5. Was für ein Auto hat Katharina? Welche Farbe?
What kind of car does Katharina own? What color?

6. Was für ein Auto hat Ludwig? Welche Farbe?
What kind of car does Ludwig own? What color?

7. Was für ein Auto hat der Reporter Tötges?
Welche Farbe?
What kind of car does reporter Tötges own? What color?

8. Was für ein Auto hat der Scheich von Kuwait?
Welche Farbe?
What kind of car does the Sheik of Kuwait own? What color?

9. Wo versteckte sich Ludwig Götten?
Where did Ludwig Götten hide?

10. Warum wurde Ludwig Götten überwacht?
Why was Ludwig Götten under observation?

11. Was für einen Beruf hat Katharina Blum?
What was Katharina Blum's profession?

12. Ist Kommissar Beizmenne ein netter freundlicher Mann?
Is inspector Beizmenne a kind friendly man?

13. Warum tragen die Polizisten Kostüme?
Why do the police wear costumes?

14. In welcher Stadt lebt Katharina?
In which city does Katharina live?

15. In welchem Jahr spielt der Film?
Which year is portrayed in the movie?

16. Was denkst du über den Reporter Tötges?
What do you think of the reporter Tötges?

17. Was ist die politische Botschaft der Geschichte?
Was ist Heinrich Bölls Absicht eine solche Geschichte
zu schreiben?
*What is the political message of the story? What is
Heinrich Böll's intention in writing such a story?*

18. Beschreibe die Handlung des Films "Die verlorene Ehre der Katharina Blum".
*Write a description of the plot of the movie "Die
verlorene Ehre der Katharina Blum".*

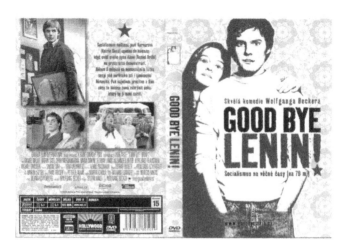

Test
Test

Name:
Name (yours):

1. Draw a drawing of your favorite scene from the movie "Goodbye Lenin!"

2. Translate into German: "Goodbye Lenin"

3. Which one is correct? Lenin's real name is ...

o   Vladimir Ilyich Ulyanov
o   Влади́мир Ильи́ч Ле́нин
o   Alexandr Kerenky
o   Count Dracula
o   Leon Trotsky
o   Eva Braun

4. Write a summary of "Goodbye Lenin!" using as many German words as you feel comfortable with.

5. The Berlin Wall came down in the year ...

o   1879
o   1899
o   1933
o   1945
o   1957
o   1972
o   1982
o   1989
o   1991
o   1998
o   2001
o   2006

6. Why would my dentist place a 4"x 4"x 6" piece of the Berlin Wall on his desk?

7. Why does mother (in the movie) have a heart attack?

8. Why does mother get blindfolded when they take her to the cabin in the woods?

9. What is the correct spelling of the name Meyer?

○ Mayer
○ Meyer
○ Mayr
○ Meyr
○ Mier
○ Myer
○ Miar
○ Liar

10. How do you see the connection between the idea of wanting to live in the past and not face the future and your own life?

11. Where does the movie take place?

12. Criticize the main actors.
A. Alex

B. Alex' sister

C. Alex' mother

189

D. Alex' girlfriend Lara

E. Detlev, the moviemaker

F. Alex' sister's boyfriend

G. Alex' dad

H. The drunken school principal

13. What is a Trabbi?

14. What is a Trabbi Kombi?

15. Why was mother afraid of Coca Cola?

16. Where did Alex' dad live?

17. What kind of music was been played at Alex' dad's house party?

18. What was the deeper meaning of this music at Alex' dad's house party?

19. If you could be in a stage adaptation of the movie "Goodbye Lenin!", which role would you want to play and why?

20. Write down a dialogue (in German) from the movie, including English subtitles ...

**21. When the Berlin Wall came down in ....
where was the West German capital then?**
o   Berlin
o   Hamburg
o   Bremen

- München
- Bonn
- Düsseldorf
- Wuppertal
- Frankfurt
- Madison
- Weimar
- Potsdam
- Rosenheim

22. Name some (at least 3, but not more than 50) of the furniture items put out on the curb (in German).

.

23. Is it true that a (East) German cosmonaut landed on the moon (on the dark side, therefore it is not known so much), before Apollo 11 circled Jupiter? And who was on board of that famous flight?

- Yes
- No
- Could have happened
- Should have happened
- It is true but the Pentagon managed to get hold of the pictures and sold them to the tiny African country of Niger in order to get some uranium (which the Secretary of State denied with the words: "I don't take the blame for my predecessors' mistakes! Next question.")
- All of the above

24. What is a "Wessi" and what is an "Ossi"?

25. What is the significance that only once did Alex not use the elevator in their apartment building and why?

26. Übersetze.

Alex fährt mit dem Taxi zu seinem Vater. Das Taxi ist ein Lada, der Taxifahrer ein früherer Kosmonaut. Alex sagt zu dem Taxifahrer: "Bitte warten Sie hier. Ich komme bald zurück." Alex' Mutter liegt im Krankenhaus. Alex' Freundin – sie heißt Lara – erzählt der Mutter die ganze Wahrheit. Alex' Vater besucht die Mutter kurz vor ihrem Tode. Alex glaubt seine Scheinwelt selbst. Er hat sich selbst überzeugt.

Translate.

Alex travels in a taxi to his father. The taxi is a "Lada", the taxi driver a former cosmonaut. Alex tells the taxi driver: "Please wait here. I will be back soon." Alex' mother is in the hospital. Alex' girl friend – her name is Lara – tells the mother the whole truth. Alex' father visits the mother shortly before her death. Alex believes in his make believe world. He has convinced himself.

Minitest

Name:

Datum:

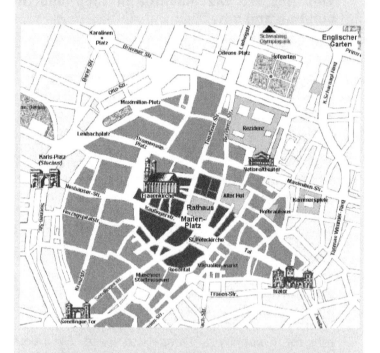

Use this map of central Munich to give directions

1. For Christmas you want to go to the Frauenkirche. After driving around in downtown Munich trying to find a parking spot for 45 minutes, you finally park at Karolinenplatz. Give directions from there to Frauenkirche.

2. After church you want to go to the Isartor for coffee. Give directions.

3. Suddenly your dog needs to do something illegal in downtown Munich, so you quickly run to the Englischer Garten park, where doggy can go into the bushes. Give directions.

4. Now - a cell phone call - you are needed at the Karlsplatz. Hurry, hurry, there's a small riot, and you are supposed to write about it for the school newspaper. Give directions.

5. Riot was a rumor, just a small demonstration by McDonald's workers who are complaining about the new ketchup, that contains GMOs. You decide to go to the Hofbräuhaus, the world famous beer hall. Give directions.

6. At the Hofbräuhaus the drunks are so plentiful, there is no way to get in, and your dog needs to go

again, so it's off to the Hofgarten, where there are some trees. Give directions.

7. After taking a nap on a park bench at the Maximilianplatz, you decide to go to Marienplatz, where you can watch the world famous Glockenspiel at the Rathaus. Give directions.

8. Continue the story.

Test

Name:

Datum:

1. Who was Otto von Bismark?

2. What were some of Otto von Bismarck's accomplishments?

3. What happened during 1914 -1918?

4. What were the events that started World War I?

5. Who fought against whom in WW I?

6. What was the "Bierhausputsch"?

7. When was the "Bierhausputsch"?

8. Who was Adolf Hitler?

9. When and how did Hitler become the leader of Germany?

10. What does "Führer" mean?

11. Was Hitler a communist?

12. When was the World War II?

13. Who were the winners of WW II?

14. How was Germany divided after WW II?

15. What are "Besatzungszonen"?

16. When was the Wall ("die Mauer") built?

17. Why was the Wall ("die Mauer") built?

18. What happened in 1989 in Germany?

19. Why do Germans want to live in America?

20. Wisconsin has a population of approx. 5 million. Germany has a population of approx.?

21. Are Germans good at ice-fishing?

22. What is the speed limit on the "Autobahn"?

23. What form of government does Germany have today?

24. Draw a map of Central Europe, showing Germany, and all countries that have a common border with Germany. Put in as many details as possible, like cities, lakes, rivers, mountains, ski lifts, etc.

A few very simple tests ...

Minitest

Name:

Datum:

Vocabulary

Light bulb   =
Outlet   =
Cable   =
Plug   =
Electricity =

Translate into German:

Susi screams: "Stop, Heribert, don't put the screwdriver into the outlet!" Two minutes later. "Oh, Heribert, your hair, your open mouth, horrible!"

List 10 words typically found in a weather report (in German):

1.   –
2.   –
3.   –
4.   –
5.   –
6.   –
7.   –
8.   –
9.   –
10. -

Minitest

Name:

Datum:

Translate:
Das Wetter ist schön. Es ist schwül, neblig, frostig, wolkig, dunstig, und stürmisch.
The weather is beautiful. It is muggy, foggy, frosty, cloudy, hazy, and stormy.

Der Regenbogen fällt von den blauen Wolken im Nebel.
The rainbow falls out of the blue clouds in the fog.

The hurricane melts the snow. The heat wave warms the cold blast.
Der Orkan schmelzt den Schnee. Die Hitzewelle wärmt die Kältewelle.

The cold air, the dry wind, the fine thunder, the fresh hail, and the clear ice, is nice.
Die kalte Luft, der trockene Wind, der feine Donner, der frische Hagel, und das klare Eis, sind nett.

The climate in Wisconsin changes from cloudburst to thunderstorm.
Das Klima in Wisconsin verändert sich vom Wolkenbruch zum Gewittersturm.

Minitest

Name:

Datum:

Give directions

Berlin to Munich:

Berlin to Hamburg:

Düsseldorf to Stuttgart:

Stuttgart to the moon:

Translate into German:

"Hi! I am Franzl. Who are you? I like your leather pants. Do you have a car with leather seats? Man, I am hungry. Where is the Pizzeria Roma? I want a cola/fanta mix, and fettuccine without everything or a dead mouse!"

"Hallo! Ich bin der Franzl. Wer bist Du? Ich liebe deine Lederhosen. Hast Du ein Auto mit Ledersitzen? Mensch, bin ich hungrig! Wo ist die Pizzeria Roma? Ich möchte ein Spezi, und Bandnudeln ohne Alles oder eine tote Maus!"

List 10 items typically found on a menu (in German):

11. –
12. –
13. –
14. –
15. –
16. –
17. –
18. –
19. –
20. –

Translate into English:

Peter und Susi rennen durch Viroqua. Sie starten an der Ecke Lintonstraße und Eisenbahnallee, dann joggen sie am Tabaklagerhaus vorbei, über die Ostallee zu der Waldorfschule, dann rechts bis zur Hauptstraße. Sie trinken Espresso im Gemeinsamer Grund Café, dann rennen sie viel schneller bis nach Westby (10 km) und zurück (10 km). Plötzlich regnet es. Blitz und Donnerschlag! Ein Orkan mit Wirbelsturm bläst von Nordwesten. Peter und Susi haben Angst. Da kommt Graf Dracula mit seiner Limosine und sagt zu Peter: "Komm mit. Ich fahre zum Friedhof. Hohohohohahaharrrr." Doch Peter ist ein Held! Er schreit: "Weg mit dir, du Höllengespenst!" Peter boxt Graf Dracula auf die Nase, und rennt mit Susi zurück nach Haus.

Peter and Susi jog through Viroqua. They start at the corner of Linton Street and Railroad Avenue, then they jog along the Tobacco Storage Building, via East Avenue to the Waldorf School, then to the right up to the Main Street. They drink espresso at the Common Ground Café, then they jog much faster to Westby (6 miles) and back (6 miles). Suddenly it rains. Lightning and thunder! A hurricane with a tornado blows from out of the Northwest. Peter and Susi are afraid. There arrives

Count Dracula in his limosine and says to Peter: "Come along. I'll drive to the cemetery. Huhuhuhuhuhoarrr." But Peter is a hero! He shouts: "Away with you, specter from hell!" Peter boxes Count Dracula on the nose, and jogs back home with Susi.

Next you will find a "multiple choice" test …

Multiblechoicequiz

(übersetzen und ankreuzen)

Viroqua ist
☐1   ein Dorf
☐2   eine Stadt
☐3   ein Misthaufen

In dem Landmarkzentrum ist
☐1   eine Schule
☐2   'ne geheime Untergrundbewegungsakademie
☐3   ein Irrenhaus

"Ich bin vom Mars und du bist ein intergalaktischer Held" bedeutet
☐1   nichts
☐2   wenig
☐3   viel

Die Viroqua Bären haben
☐1   zwei Mopeds
☐2   einen Briefkasten
☐3   eine Höhle

Wer ist Helmuth?
☐1   Theo's Onkel
☐2   Conrad's Bruder
☐3   Heribert's Freund

Wo wohnt Susi?
☐3   Überall
☐1   Ich weiß es, aber ich halte es geheim, weil ich Susi heimlich liebe
☐2   in der Leopoldstraße 134

Wieviel ist zweihundertfünfundvierzig und ½ geteilt durch dreiundsechzig?
□3   Mein Rechner ist kaputt. Schade!
□2   drei komma acht neun sechs acht zwei fünf drei etc.
□1   Frage doch die Maus

Warum sind wir hier?
□2   Schlechtes Karma
□3   Weil heute Freitag ist
□1   Ich weiß nicht. Frage meinen Freund Piet.

Wieviel dumme Fragen gibt es in dem Universum?
□1   eine
□2   Was?
□3   Es gibt mehr Fragen als Antworten

Das Haar ist
□2   auf dem Kopf
□3   auf dem Fuss
□1   auf der Tür

Der Finger ist
□1   an der Hand
□3   ein Scheibenwischer
□2   an dem Arm

"Ich bin ich und du bist du" bedeutet
□2   nichts
□3   wenig
□1   viel

Der Viroqua Supermarkt hat
□1   ein Moped
□2   einen Briefkasten
□3   viel Eiskrem

Wer ist Heribert?

☐1   Theo's Onkel
☐3   Conrad's Bruder
☐2   Conrad's Freund

Wo wohnts du?

☐1   Überall
☐2   Ich weiß es nicht
☐3   _____

Wieviel Haare hat der Mensch?

☐3   Zweiunddreizig
☐2   Fünfhunderzweiundachtzigtausenddreihundertneunundsiebzig
☐1   Frage doch die Maus

Wieviel dumme Fragen gibt es in dem Universum?

☐1   Zwei
☐3   Wie?
☐2   Es gibt mehr Fragen als Antworten

Auswertung (addiere deine Punktzahl):
0-17 Punkte: **Du weisst sehr viel**
18-28 Punkte: **Du weisst zu viel**
29-51 Punkte: **Du bist sehr weise**
über 52 Punkte: **Du kannst nicht rechnen**

Multible choice quiz (select all that apply)

(translate and chose)

Viroqua is
☐1   a village
☐2   a city
☐3   a manure heap

In the Landmark Center (school building) there is
☐1   a school
☐2   a secret underground movement academy
☐3   an insane asylum

"I am from mars and you are an inter galactic hero" means
☐1   nothing
☐2   little
☐3   much

The bears of Viroqua have
☐1   two Mopeds
☐2   one mailbox
☐3   one cave

Who is Helmuth?
☐1   Theo's uncle
☐2   Conrad's brother
☐3   Heribert's friend

Where does Susi live?
☐3   Everywhere
☐1   I know it, but I'll keep it secret, because I am secretly in love with Susi
☐2   at Leopoldstraße 134

How much is 245 ½ divided by 63?
☐3   My calculator is broken. Pity!
☐2   3.8968253 ...
☐1   Ask the mouse

Why are we here?
☐2   Bad karma
☐3   Because today is Friday
☐1   I don't know. Ask my friend Piet.

How many stupid questions are there in the universe?

☐1　One
☐2　What?
☐3　There are more questions than answers

The hair is
☐2　on the head
☐3　on the foot
☐1　on the door

The finger is
☐1　on the hand
☐3　a windshield wiper
☐2　on the arm

"I am me and you are you" means
☐2　nothing
☐3　little
☐1　much

The Viroqua Supermarket has
☐1　a Moped
☐2　a mailbox
☐3　lots of ice cream

Who is Heribert?
☐1　Theo's uncle
☐3　Conrad's brother
☐2　Conrad'sfriend

Where do you live?
☐1　Everywhere
☐2　I don't know
☐3　_____

How many hairs has the human being?
☐3　32
☐2　582,379
☐1　Ask the mouse

How many stupid questions are there in the universe?
□1   Two
□3   What?
□2   There are more questions than answers

Result (add up your points):
0-17 points: You know very much
18-28 points: You know too much
29-51 points: You are very wise
over 52 points: You can't do the math

And now the ever popular psychological evaluation camouflaged as a test ... teenagers love this one in particular.

Psycho-Test für Deutschschüler

1.   Wie heißt du?
a.   (3 Punkte)

2.   Wie alt bist du?
a.   (0 Punkte)   12
b.   (1 Punkt)   14
c.   (2 Punkte)   15
d.   (3 Punkte)   16
e.   (4 Punkte)   über 16

3.   Wo wohnst du?
a.   (0 Punkte)   Ich weiß nicht
b.   (1 Punkt)   In Viroqua
c.   (2 Punkte)   Nicht in Viroqua
d.   (3 Punkte)   In einem Haus
e.   (4 Punkte)   In einem Zelt

4.   Was magst du essen?
a.   (0 Punkte)   Pommes Frites
b.   (1 Punkt)   Pizza-Mann Pizza
c.   (2 Punkte)   Schokoladeneis
d.   (3 Punkte)   Wiener Schnitzel
e.   (4 Punkte)   Tofu-Hamburger

5.   Wohin möchtest du reisen?
a.   (0 Punkte)   nirgendwo
b.   (1 Punkt)   nach La Crosse
c.   (2 Punkte)   nach Kanada
d.   (3 Punkte)   Deutschland
e.   (4 Punkte)   Bayern

6. Was für ein Auto magst du?
a.   (0 Punkte)   Smart Car
b.   (1 Punkt)   Opel
c.   (2 Punkte)   Mercedes
d.   (3 Punkte)   BMW
e.   (4 Punkte)   Audi
f.   (5 Punkte)   Fahrrad

7. Was ist deine Lieblingsfarbe?
a.   (0 Punkte)   weiß
b.   (1 Punkt)   schwarz
c.   (2 Punkte)   grün
d.   (3 Punkte)   gelb
e.   (4 Punkte)   rot

8. Welchen Sport magst du?
a.   (0 Punkte)   Kanu
b.   (1 Punkt)   Rennen
c.   (2 Punkte)   Schlafen
d.   (3 Punkte)   Fußball
e.   (4 Punkte)   Tischtennis
f.   (5 Punkte)   Minigolf

9. Welchen Beruf magst du?
a.   (0 Punkte)   Nachtwächter(in)
b.   (1 Punkt)   Bedienung
c.   (2 Punkte)   Sänger(in)
d.   (3 Punkte)   Lehrer(in)
e.   (4 Punkte)   Bauer (Bäuerin)

10. Wie sieht dein(e) Traumfrau (Traummann) aus?
a.   (0 Punkte)   lieb, nett, hübsch
b.   (1 Punkt)   anders
c.   (2 Punkte)   interessant
d.   (3 Punkte)   total egal
e.   (4 Punkte)   ich weiß nicht

11. Welches Tier magst du am liebsten?
a.   (0 Punkte)   Deutscher Schäferhund
b.   (1 Punkt)   Waschbär
c.   (2 Punkte)   schwarzweiße Kuh
d.   (3 Punkte)   Pferd
e.   (4 Punkte)   Gorilla

12. Welche Musik magst du am liebsten?
a.   (0 Punkte)   Volksmusik
b.   (1 Punkt)   Klassische Musik
c.   (2 Punkte)   Wasserfall
d.   (3 Punkte)   Walzer
e.   (4 Punkte)   Technopunkrockreggae

Auswertung:
0-12   **Du bist ein freundlicher Mensch**
13-24   **Du bist normal**
25-36   **Du bist ein bißchen frech**
37-48   **Du bist ein wilder Typ**
49+   **Du bist gefährlich**

217

Psycho-Test for German Students

1. What's your name?
a.   (3 Points)

2. How old are you?
a.   (0 Points)   12
b.   (1 Point)   14
c.   (2 Points)   15
d.   (3 Points)   16
e.   (4 Points)   over 16

3. Where do you live?
a.   (0 Points)   I don't know
b.   (1 Point)   In Viroqua
c.   (2 Points)   Not in Viroqua
e.   (3 Points)   In a house
f.   (4 Points)   In a tent

4. What do you like to eat?
a.   (0 Points)   French fries
b.   (1 Point)   Pizza-Mann Pizza
c.   (2 Points)   Chocolate ice cream
d.   (3 Points)   Veal cutlet Viennese
e.   (4 Points)   Tofu-Hamburger

5. Where to do you want to travel?
a.   (0 Points)   nowhere
b.   (1 Point)   to La Crosse
c.   (2 Points)   to Kanada
d.   (3 Points)   Germany
e.   (4 Points)   Bavaria

6. What kind of car do you like?
a.   (0 Points)   Smart Car
b.   (1 Point)   Opel
c.   (2 Points)   Mercedes
d.   (3 Points)   BMW
e.   (4 Points)   Audi
f.   (5 Points)   Bicycle

7.   What is your favorite color?
a.   (0 Points)   white
b.   (1 Point)   black
c.   (2 Points)   green
d.   (3 Points)   yellow
e.   (4 Points)   red

8.   Which sport do you like?
a.   (0 Points)   Canoeing
b.   (1 Point)   Jogging
c.   (2 Points)   Sleeping
d.   (3 Points)   Soccer
e.   (4 Points)   Table tennis
f.   (5 Points)   Minigolf

9.   Which profession do you like?
a.   (0 Points)   Night watchman
b.   (1 Point)   Waiter (waitress)
c.   (2 Points)   Singer
d.   (3 Points)   Teacher
e.   (4 Points)   Farmer

10.   How do you imagine your ideal partner?
a.   (0 Points)   lovely, nice, cute
b.   (1 Point)   different
c.   (2 Points)   interesting
d.   (3 Points)   makes no difference
e.   (4 Points)   I don't know

11.   Which animal do you like best?
a.   (0 Points)   German shepherd
b.   (1 Point)   Racoon
c.   (2 Points)   black and white cow
d.   (3 Points)   Horse
e.   (4 Points)   Gorilla

12. What kind of music do you like best?
a.   (0 Points)   Folklore
b.   (1 Point)   Classical music
c.   (2 Points)   Waterfall
d.   (3 Points)   Waltz
e.   (4 Points)   Technopunkrockreggae

Results:
0-12   **You are a friendly human being**
13-24   **You are normal**
25-36   **You are a little impudent**
37-48   **You are a wild type**
49+   **You are dangerous**

A test which tests the knowledge concerning the USA ...

Kennst Du die USA? Ein Wissenstest.
Do you know the USA? Test your knowledge.

Wie heißt der tiefste Punkt der USA?
What is the name of the lowest point in the USA?
- ❑   Death Valley   0
- ❑   Deep Throat
- ❑   Hollow Well

Sind die Vereinigten Staaten?
Are the United States?
- ❑   Kleiner als China
- ❑   *Smaller than China*
- ❑   Genauso groß wie China
- ❑   *Same size as China*
- ❑   Größer als China   0
- ❑   *Bigger than China*   *0*

Wie heißt der höchste Berg?
What is the name of the highest mountain?
- ❑   Mount Helens
- ❑   Battle Mountain
- ❑   Mount McKinley   0

Was versteht man unter "Hispanic"?
What is meant by „Hispanic"?
- ❑   Ein Drink mit Tequila
- ❑   *A drink with Tequila*
- ❑   Ein Spanier der Englisch spricht
- ❑   *A Spaniard who speaks English*

❏   Ein Einwanderer aus Lateinamerika 0
❏   *An immigrant from Latin America 0*

Wie viele Einwohner haben die USA?
How many people live in the USA?
❏   Circa 278 Millionen   0
❏   Circa 295 Millionen
❏   Circa 261 Millionen

Aus wie viel Bundesstaaten bestehen die USA?
How many federal states make up the USA?
❏   49
❏   50   0
❏   56

Welches ist der wichtigste Feiertag?
Which is the most important holiday?
❏   Thanksgiving Day
❏   Labor Day
❏   4. Juli   0

Ist das jährliche Pro-Kopf-Einkommen?
Is the per capita income
❏   höher als in Kanada   0
❏   *higher than in Canada*   *0*
❏   niedriger als in Kanada
❏   *lower than in Canada*
❏   genauso hoch wie in Kanada
❏   *the same as in Canada*

Wann wurde die amerikanische Verfassung
geschrieben?
When was the american constitution created?
❏   1776
❏   1787   0
❏   1791

Minitest

Bitte nenne die Länder auf Deutsch...
Please name the countries in German

1.
2.
3.
4.
5.
6.
7.
8.
9.
10.
11.
12.
13.
14.
15.
16.

Finally, a rather long test that is especially suited to be used at the end of a semester or block in order to determine and evaluate the progress that each student has made during the semester or block ...

Großer Test
Big Test

Name:
Name:

Datum:
Date:

Bitte übersetzen, und/oder die Fragen beantworten; anderenfalls bitte die Anweisungen befolgen.
Please translate, and/or answer the questions; or follow the instructions somehow.

1. "Wieviel Uhr ist es?" has the same meaning as
☐ Wie spät ist es?   0
☐ Wieviel Zeit ist es?
☐ Wie late ist es?

2. Draw a digital clock that shows: Zwölf Uhr fünfzehn

3.   Draw a grandfather's clock that shows: Viertel nach Acht

4.   Wieviel Euros kostet eine Tasse Tee mit Milch?

☐   € 65,90

☐   € 5,90

☐   € 1,90   0

5.   How many liters of gasoline will fit into the tank of a 2002 BMW 525 tii turbo?

☐   40

☐   60   0

☐   70

6.   Was bedeutet "Ich bin ein Berliner"?

What is the meaning of "Ich bin ein Berliner"?

☐   Je suis un Berlinois   0

☐   I am a citizen of the fine city of Berlin or one of the surrounding boroughs   0

☐   I am a jelly doughnut which can be purchased for € 1,90   0

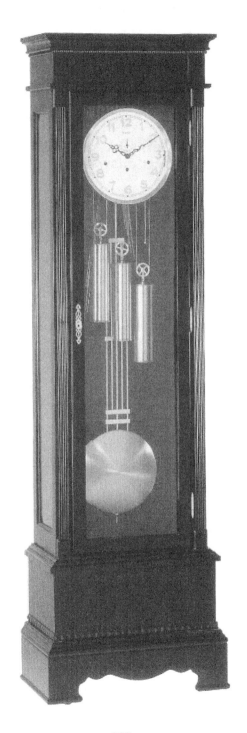

227

7. Translate: Why doesn't the cow like the coffee?

Warum mag die Kuh den Kaffee nicht?

7A. How do Germans say hello to each other (check all correct answers).

☐	Servus	0
☐	Grüß Gott	0
☐	Hallo	0
☐	Tschüss	
☐	Güle Güle	
☐	(Silence)	
☐	How are you there in Westby?	
☐	Hi	
☐	Om	
☐	Bonjour	
☐	Guten Tag	0
☐	Ciao	
☐	Heh Alter	
☐	Na du	
☐	Du bist blöd	

Name in German:

8.   The days of the week

Name in German:

9.   The 4 seasons

10.   4 drinks

11.   4 things to eat

12.   4 things to wear

13.   4 body parts

14.   4 animals

Name in German:

15.   4 cars

16.   Capitals of Germany, Austria, Switzerland, and Wisconsin

17.   4 rivers

18.   4 spices

19.   4 cities

20.   7 colors

21.   10 numbers

22.   Übersetze
Translate

Unterhalb der Stadt Viroqua gibt es eine große Bärenhöhle. In der Höhle wohnen achtundsiebzig Bären. Die Bären sind schlau. Sie haben ein kleines Restaurant, wo sie Honig und Blaubeeren essen. Zwei der Bären heissen Heribert und Dagobert. Dagobert ist ein Mopedrennfahrer und Heribert ein superschneller Skateboarder. Am Mittwoch rasen Heribert und Dagobert zu dem Supermarkt. Sie wollen Bier und Limonade kaufen. Heribert hat zwanzig Euro Taschengeld, aber Dagobert ist leider pleite. Heribert trinkt Limonade und frißt (fressen = to eat like an animal) zweihundertvierundzwanzig Skittles. Dagobert sitzt daneben und lacht nicht. Dann geht Heribert ins Kino. Er sieht einen Film namens "Dude – wo ist mein Moped?" Dagobert wandert über den Parkplatz und ist sauer. Endlich ist der Film zu Ende und die zwei Bären fahren wieder nach Hause.

Underneath the city of Viroqua there is a huge bear cave. In the cave there live 78 bears. The bears are clever. They run a little restaurant, where they eat honey and blueberries. Two of the bears are named Heribert and Dagobert. Dagobert is a moped racer and Heribert a superfast skateboarder. On Wednesday Heribert and Dagobert race to the supermarket. They want to buy beer and lemonade. Heribert has 20 Euros in pocket money, but Dagobert is unfortunately bankrupt. Heribert drinks lemonade and wolfs down 224 Skittles. Dagobert sits next to him and does not laugh. Then Heribert goes to the movies. He watches the movie "Dude – Where is My Moped?" Dagobert wanders across the parking lot in a dark mood. Finally the movie ends and the two bears ride back home.

23.   Identify and describe in German objects in this picture.

24.   Name (in German) as many items on the picture as you can. Describe them, show location on painting.
Example: (1) Die Sonne ist gelb.
The sun is yellow

25. Translate the vocabulary

rechts	right
links	left
geradeaus	straight ahead
um die Ecke	around the corner
gegenüber	opposite
immer der Nase nach	follow your nose
umsteigen	change (trains)
nehmen	to take
fahren	to drive
der Bus	bus
der Zug	train
die U- (S-) Bahn	subway (city) train
die Haltestelle	stop
das Flugzeug	airplane
das Taxi	taxi
der Pfeffer	pepper
der Paprika	paprika
der Zimt	cinnamon
der Ingwer	ginger
der Cardamom	cardamon
der Koriander	coriander
der Safran	saffron
die Muskatnuss	nutmeg
die Nelken	allspice
das Basilikum	basil
das Anis	anise
die Vanille	vanilla
der Kümmel	caraway
die Lorbeerblätter	bay leaves
die Chilis	chillies
der Knoblauch	garlic
der Oregano	oregano
die Senfkörner	mustard seed
die Zwiebel	onion
der Estragon	tarragon

essen (esse, ißt, ißt, essen, eßt, essen) – to eat
trinken (trinke, trinkst, trinkt, trinken, trinkt, trinken) – to drink

das Restaurant, die Restaurants
restaurant

das Wirtshaus, die Wirtshäuser
tavern

das Café, die Cafes
café

der Kaffee, die Kaffees
coffee

der Tee, die Tees
tea

die Speisekarte,n
menu

der Nachtisch, die Nachtische
dessert

der Kellner, die Kellner, die Kellnerin, die Kellner-
innen
waiter, waitress

die Bedienung, en
server

das Kalbfleisch, die Kalbfleische
veal

das Schweinefleisch, die Schweinefleische
pork

das Hammelfleisch, die Hammelfleische
mutton

der Braten, die Braten
roast

das Kotelett, die Koteletts
cutlet

der Sojaburger, die Sojaburgers
soy burger

die Wurst, die Würste
sausage

das Hühnerfleisch, die Hühnerfleische
chicken (meat)

der Salat, die Salate
salad

das Gewürz, die Gewürze
spice

das Rührei, die Rühreier
scrambled egg

das Spiegelei, die Spiegeleier
fried egg

die Scheibe, die Scheiben
slice

das Gebäck, die Gebäcke
pastry

die Getreideflocken
cereal flakes

der Kartoffelbrei, die Kartoffelbreie
mashed potatoes

die Schokolade, n
chocolate

der Hering, die Heringe
herring

durchgebraten
well done

saftig
juicy

verfault
rotten

schmackhaft
tasty

geschmacklos
tasteless

köstlich
delicious

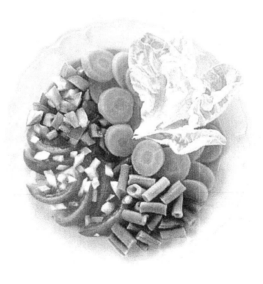

"Will there be anything left for Christmas presents?"

26. Draw a cartoon.

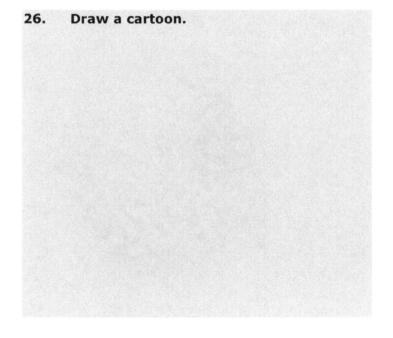

27. Write down a conversation in German.

28. **Write a story in German.**

Germans Are Funny

Chapter 10: *Der Kurs (Course Announcement)*

The announcement of each course offered should include a short description of the course, requirements for passing, expectations of the students, and supplies lists.

German Class (Deutschunterricht)

"Erst die Arbeit, dann das Vergnügen"
"First all the work needs to get done, then perhaps we'll have some fun"

German class will be offered again for the school year ... . Please see and study the following course description and requirements for passing the class, **before** signing up for this course.

In this class, students will be expected to study and apply themselves, to create a beautiful Schönschriftheft™ (Main Lesson Book style booklet or folder), and to prepare and give a presentation to the class. A minimum of 2 hours per week of homework, study of vocabulary, working on projects, preparing for classes, or working on special assignments, will be expected. Classes are on Mondays, Wednesdays and Fridays. Homework and assignments will be given on Mondays (due on Wednesdays) and Wednesdays (due on Fridays), but not on Fridays (in order to keep the weekend free of school work for students who keep up with their assignments during the week).

Two basic courses will be offered: **(1) German for Beginners and Intermediate Level**, and **(2) Advanced German**.

Students applying to enter the advanced level, need to have fulfilled a minimum of 3 semesters (or equivalent) of high school German, need to be highly motivated, need to be able to work independently at times, and will be expected to be available for some student teaching to the beginners/intermediate level class.

Students interested in participating in the **foreign student exchange program** with our sister school, the ... in Germany, need to have fulfilled a minimum of 3 semesters (or equivalent) of high school German, need to be highly motivated, and need to have passing grades of "Pass with Honors" for a minimum of 2 semesters.

Supplies. Supplies needed for these courses include:
1. German—English dictionary (*Langenscheidt* is recommended)
2. Pens and pencils
3. Paper
4. Ringbinder (1/2")
5. Colored pencils
6. Gute Laune *(good mood)*

Langenscheidt's
Compact
Dictionary

German

German-English
English-German

Germans Are Funny

Chapter 11: *Die Noten (Grades)*

Grades should not replace the important narrative reports that the teachers in Waldorf schools so diligently create at the end of each school year. In the high school setting it is advisable to add a grading system to the narrative report routine. The students are now old enough to be able to deal with and learn from the presence of grades. Whether we use the A B C F grading system familiar to people in the USA, or – for cultural diversity reasons – introduce the grading system of choice in Germany, or another system, or perhaps a hybrid, the main point is that we work with it in creative ways. Following, you will find a system used in my courses, which can easily be adjusted to different situations.

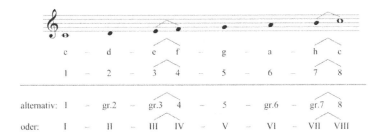

Grades and requirements for successfully or unsuccessfully completing a semester of German class

Noten und Bedingungen für ein erfolgreiches oder nicht erfolgreiches Abschneiden pro Halbjahr im Deutschunterricht

Grades:
A - Pass w/Honors
B - Pass
C - Pass
F - Fail
N - Not attended

Noten:
1 - Sehr gut
2 – Gut
3 – Befriedigend
4 – Ausreichend
5 – Mangelhaft
6 - Ungenügend
N - Nicht teilgenommen

Attendance:
A - 80+ %
B/C - 50+ %
N - 49% or less

Anwesenheit:
1 - 80+ %
2/3/4 - 50+ %
N - 49 % oder weniger

Homework:
A - 100%
B/C - 80+ %
F - 79% or less

Hausaufgaben:
1 - 100 %
2/3/4 - 80+ %
5/6 - 79% oder weniger

Tests/quizzes:
A – 80+%
B/C - 50% - 79%
F - 49% or less

Tests/Quize:
1 - 80+ %
2/3/4 - 50% - 79%
5/6 - 49% oder weniger

Schönschriftheft
A - All entries neatly done
B/C - 80+%
F - 79% or less, or book disappeared

Main Lesson Book type booklet:
1 - Alle Eintragungen schön und sauber
2/3/4 - 80+ %
5/6 - 79% oder weniger, oder das Heft ist ver-
schwunden

Presentations:
A - 1 well done
B/C - 1 done
F - None done

Präsentationen:
1 - Eine hervorragend durchgeführt
2/3/4 - Eine durchgeführt
5/6 - Keine durchgeführt

Class participation:
A - Attentive and participatory
B/C – Mostly present
F - Mostly asleep or chatting in English

Unterrichtsteilnahme:
1 - Aufmerksam und teilnehmend
2/3/4 - Meistens anwesend
5/6 - Meistens am Schlafen oder am Schwätzen (auf
Englisch)

Behavior:
A - Pleasant and cheerful and/or serious and meaningful
B/C - Neutral, but no blank stare
F - Mean, disruptive, and swearing in English

Verhalten:
1 - Nett und fröhlich und/oder ernst und tiefschürfend
2/3/4 - Neutral, aber ohne dummes Glotzen
5/6 - Gemein, störend, und fluchend (auf Englisch)

Chapter 12: *Der Wochenbericht (Weekly Reports)*

"Considering your C grade in Geography - you won't get far!"

Reports are another important way of communication. The parents of your students, but also the students themselves, appreciate frequent reports concerning their status in the class, and the progress made. Ideally weekly reports are being sent home to each family; depending on the circumstances, bi-weekly, or monthly reports might suffice. Following you will find some examples of weekly reports.

Student Report/Schülerfortschrittsbericht 1

German Class/Deutschunterricht
Teacher/Lehrer: Conrad Rehbach
Date/Datum:

We worked this month on a variety of themes including Tagebuch (diary), poetry by Goethe, Wetterbericht (weather reports), sayings and proverbs, superlative rules, conjugations, one mini test, and continued the "Adventures of Heribert" Series.

Student/Schüler: A ... (Level 4)

A is keeping up with the work quite well – there is one missing homework (Harfenspieler poem translation/interpretation) due at this point.

Student/Schüler: B ... (Level 3)

B did not hand in any homework, in fact I did not see him at school at all lately!
(This student is on a foreign exchange in Germany!)
Student/Schüler: C ... (Level 2)

C has all work in. C has a good feel for the correct spelling of German words.

Student/Schüler: D ... (Level 2)

D has absent this Friday. So he has not handed in the homework for this day. Otherwise all is fine.

Student/Schüler: E ... (Level 1)

All work in and everything is fine.

Student Report/Schülerfortschrittsbericht 2

German Class/Deutschunterricht
Teacher/Lehrer: Conrad Rehbach
Date/Datum:

We continued to start each class with putting entries into the *Tagebuch* (diary). We studied how to describe pictures, and continued with restaurant and food related vocabulary, numbers, spelling, and played blackboard scrabble. We had a number of translation exercises, dictations and various homework assignments, some related to the Main Lesson courses.

Entries for the *Schönschriftheft™*
(Main Lesson Book equivalent):
#1: Speisekarte;
#2 Der Edle Achtgliedrige Pfad.

Each student will be required to do one presentation to the class per semester.

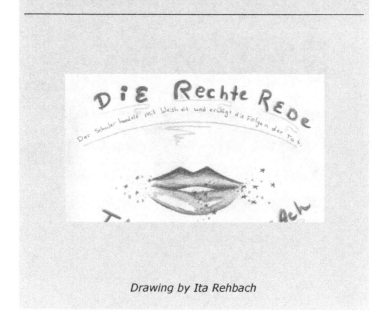

Drawing by Ita Rehbach

256

Student/Schüler: A ... (Level 4)

- Homework: (2 missing) Koran translation and Monet picture description
- Presentation for the semester: A fulfilled his presentation requirement summa cum laude with his presentation on Johann Sebastian Bach
- Mini test result (22 Sep): 69% = Gut
- Test result (26 Oct): 100% = Sehr gut

Overall: Doing great in class

Student/Schüler: B ... (Level 3)

- Homework: O.K.
- Presentation for the semester: In the works – so I hope
- Mini test result (22 Sep): 70% = Gut
- Test result (26 Oct): 50% = Befriedigend

Overall: B does his work usually quite well, except for his homework, which was done very well recently. He seems to excel at doing assignments at 2:30 AM (which he emails to me at 3:05 AM ...), but so far he manages to stay awake in class.

Student/Schüler: C ... (Level 3)

- Homework: O.K.
- Presentation for the semester: In the works, no?
- Mini test result (22 Sep): 72% = Gut
- Test result (26 Oct): 100% = Sehr gut

Overall: Nice job with homework. C is the Scrabblemeister.

Student Report/Schülerfortschrittsbericht 3

German Class/Deutschunterricht
Teacher/Lehrer: Conrad Rehbach
Date/Datum:

This week we continued with poetry by Johann Wolfgang von Goethe, continued with the daily diary, had a dictation and translation exercises, and continued working on the *Schönschriftheft™* (equivalent to a Main Lesson Book) for the spring semester.

Schönschriftheft™ entry #1: Collage about animals
Schönschriftheft™ entry #2: Gedicht/poem: Fisch Tisch Haus Maus
Schönschriftheft™ entry #3: Gedicht/poem: Der Zauberlehrling

Student/Schüler: A ... (Level 1)

- Homework: one missing – Komet picture description
- Presentation for the semester: In the works, yes?
- Mini test result (22 Sep): 24% = acceptable
- Test result (26 Oct): 30% = acceptable

Overall: A seems frustrated at time. Don't despair! German is a difficult language, and needs a lot of practice, but so does playing *Eishockey*.

Student/Schüler: B ... (Level 1)

- Homework: O.K.
- Presentation for the semester: In the works, perhaps?
- Mini test result (22 Sep): 48% = not bad
- Test result (26 Oct): 100% = Sehr gut

Overall: B does all her work well and on time. She is ready to move up a level or two in no time. Schön!

Student/Schüler: C ... (Level 1)

- Homework: O.K.
- Presentation for the semester: Plan submitted
- Mini test result (22 Sep): Not attended
- Test result (26 Oct): 20% = Can do better

Overall: C is handing in his assignments on time and well done. He tries to keep up with the class. He is quiet but pays attention. Gut.

Student/Schüler: D ... (Level 4)

D taught a lesson on Friday. He gave a well prepared presentation about the 4 cases and their usage. He led the students well, answered questions, solicited participation, and had the students work on an exercise. Well done!

Student/Schüler: E ... (Level 4)

Presentation requirement fulfilled? - Not yet!!
Schönschriftheft* done? - Perhaps.
Homework assignments? - 0 missing.
On the road to passing this class? - Hopefully yes.

Student Report/Schülerfortschrittsbericht 4

German Class/Deutschunterricht
Teacher/Lehrer: Conrad Rehbach
Date/Datum:

This week we continued with the daily diary, had translation exercises, and continued working on the *Schönschriftheft™* (equivalent to a Main Lesson Book) for the spring semester. A new set of vocabulary words ("internal combustion engines") was introduced; we started on a new drawing for the Schönschriftheft, and we listened to student presentations.

Schönschriftheft™ Spring semester entry #1:
Collage about animals
Schönschriftheft™ Spring semester entry #2:
Gedicht/poem: Fisch Tisch Haus Maus
Schönschriftheft™ Spring semester entry #3:
Gedicht/poem: Der Zauberlehrling
Schönschriftheft™ Spring semester entry #4:
Gedicht/poem: Die Chemie
Schönschriftheft™ Spring semester entry #5:
Zeichnung/drawing: Der Motor

Grades:
Sehr gut = very good = A
Gut = good = B
Befriedigend = satisfactory = C
Ausreichend = sufficient = C-
Mangelhaft = insufficient = F
Ungenügend = unacceptable = F

Student/Schüler: A ... (Level 3)

Presentation requirement fulfilled? - Not yet!!
Schönschriftheft* done? - Perhaps.
Homework assignments? - 2 missing.
On the road to passing this class? - Possibly yes.

Student/Schüler: B ... (Level 2)

Presentation requirement fulfilled? - Not yet!!
Schönschriftheft* done? - Perhaps.
Homework assignments? - 2 missing.
On the road to passing this class? - Most likely.

Student/Schüler: C ... (Level 2)

Presentation requirement fulfilled? - Not yet!!
Schönschriftheft* done? - Perhaps.
Homework assignments? - 1 missing.
On the road to passing this class? - There is hope.

Student/Schüler: D ... (Level 2)

D gave her presentation for this semester on the "Hindenburg". She had a picture, and some original text concerning the crash of the Hindenburg in New Jersey. The presentation was engaging and well done; D has a good presence in front of the class, and interacted in a great way with her audience, giving relevant facts, and answering questions posed by the students.

- Homework: O.K.
- Presentation for the semester: Completed (Sehr gut).
- Mini test result (16 Jan): 86% = Gut
- Mini test result (21 Feb): 96% = Sehr gut

Germans Are Funny

Chapter 13: *Der Semesterbericht (Semester Reports)*

At the end of each semester (or in a block system, at the end of each block) a comprehensive narrative report is due, which should include a course description, a narrative evaluation, grades and attendance records.

Example of a Semester Report

Part 1 – Course Description

German as a Foreign Language is offered at the ...... High School as a four-year program. Students can fulfill their foreign language requirements (for college admission, etc.) by successfully advancing through this foreign language course. Students are being admitted into the program without prior (or with very little) knowledge of the German language. Students advance through year one to four. Students with prior knowledge and study of the German language, can be admitted into the appropriate level.
The aim of this German class is to use and expand a basic working knowledge of German vocabulary, understanding the basics of the German grammar,

and becoming familiar with the geography and culture of the German speaking countries in Central Europe.

The students learn the basics of conversation in German, and practice the spoken language skills with the aid of poems by classical and modern German poets, by reciting text material, by learning and practicing dialogue, and through general conversations in class. Writing skills are being learned via numerous exercises, some structured, some more free, allowing for creativity, and working with the same basic vocabulary, and slowly but constantly adding new German words, phrases, and expressions. The learning of the German grammar is done with presentations and exercises, drawing on the familiar vocabulary previously given, and studied. Grammar work includes the use of the articles, plurals, declinations according to the four cases (Nominativ, Genetiv, Dativ, Akkusativ), sentence structure, questions, commands, negation, and the conjugation of verbs in the present tense, past tense, and future tense.

The students are presented with and study German poetry, excerpts from texts, little fictional stories, sayings and proverbs, newspaper texts, and German expressions, concerning the immediate surroundings, the colors, time, numbers, the alphabet, days, planets, months, seasons, money, food, clothing, names of cities and important landmarks, and common activities with an emphasis on travel.

Part 2 - Individual Student Evaluations

Example I

Student: A ...
Course: German
Teacher: Conrad Rehbach
Year/Level 1 (1 – 4)
Sessions: 44
Attended: 40 (91%)
Grade: Pass with Honors

A's overall performance during the fall semester was very good; at the end of the semester A had all homework assignments completed, and he had good results concerning the tests. A was attentive and participated very well in class. A has a natural ability to learn languages and his pronunciation and spelling are quite good. Given more intensive study of the vocabulary, A could possible go "undercover" in Amishland, and successfully pretend to be from Germany. A's *Schönschriftheft*™ although not ready for exhibition at the Art Institute of Liberty Pole, was complete, put together with care and included some beautiful work. A chose to do a presentation by creating and showing a well-received movie starring himself and his siblings titled "Ich Chef Du Nichts", which won Fall Semester Golden Globe Award for best director, most original plot twist, and superb acting. The movie was interesting, and fun to watch.

Example II

Student: B ...
Course: German
Teacher: Conrad Rehbach
Year/Level 1 (1 – 4)
Sessions: 44
Attended: 42 (96%)
Grade: Pass with Honors

B's overall performance during the spring semester was very good; at the end of the semester B had completed all homework assignments. B had good to very good results concerning the tests. B chose to do a presentation to the class about the Alpine yodel trio the "Ursprungbuam" which included a brief history of yodeling, and gave the class the opportunity to listen to some of the finest yodeling ever recorded. B was very attentive, and enjoyed participating in class; her behavior was impeccable at all times.

Example III

Student: C ...
Course: German
Teacher: Conrad Rehbach
Year/Level 3 (1 – 4)
Sessions: 44
Attended: 43 (98%)
Grade: Pass with Honors

C's overall performance during the fall semester was very good. C's attendance was close to 100%, and he scored 100% concerning his homework, which fulfilled this requirement. He scored well above average in the tests. Cf's *Schönschriftheft*™ was complete, and beautifully done. C chose a presentation on the German prime minister "Gerhard Schröder", which was well prepared and delivered. C was extremely attentive, and participated eagerly in class; his behavior was without fault at all times.

Example IV

Student: D ...
Course: German
Teacher: Conrad Rehbach
Year/Level 4 (1 – 4)
Sessions: 44
Attended: 37 (84%)
Grade: Pass

D's overall performance during the fall semester was good; at the end of the semester D had all homework assignments completed, and she had adequate to very good results concerning the tests. D was attentive and participated in class. D has the ability to learn languages, and her pronunciation and spelling are getting better. Given more intensive study of the vocabulary, D will do well in the future. D's *Schönschriftheft*™, although not ready for exhibition at the Viroqua Food Coop, as it shows signs of being completed in a hasty fashion, was complete, and included some beautiful drawings. D chose to do a presentation about the German politician "Petra Kelly". The presentation was well prepared and included relevant material brought to the class' attention via a narrative supplemented by visual aids.

Example V

Student: E ...
Course: German
Teacher: Conrad Rehbach
Year/Level 2 (1 – 4)
Sessions: 44
Attended: 39 (87%)
Grade: Pass

E's overall performance during the fall semester was very good; at the end of the semester, E had all homework assignments completed, and she had excellent results concerning the tests. E was attentive and participated very well in class. E has a natural ability to learn languages, and her pronunciation and spelling are quite good. Given more intensive study of the vocabulary, E will do very well at her planned foreign exchange visit to Germany next fall. E's *Schönschriftheft*™, although not ready for exhibition at the Art Institute of Mason City (Iowa) as it shows signs of being completed in a hasty fashion, had all required entries, and included some beautiful poetry. E chose to do a presentation about the German writer "Franz Kafka". The presentation was well prepared, and included relevant material brought to the class' attention via a narrative, and supplemented by a visual (powerpoint) presentation.

E has to increase the time spent on studying vocabulary, and work with more care and attention to details.

Franz Kafka 1883–1924

Bibliography

Bly, Robert, James Hillman and Michael Meade. *The Rag and Bone Shop of the Heart.* New York: HarperCollins, 1993.

Diehl, Margrit. *German is Fun, Book 2.* New York: Amsco School Publications, 1999.

Huebener, Theodore. *A First Course in German.* Lexington, MA: D. C. Heath and Company, 1973.

Jannach, Hubert. *German for Reading Knowledge. New York: American Book Company, 1961.*

Lindenberg, Christoph. *Teaching History. Suggested Themes for the Curriculum in Waldorf Schools.* Great Barrington, MA: Association of Waldorf Schools of North America, 1989.

Mastervision. *Basic German and Russian by DVD.* New York: Mastervision, 2005.

Nelson, Jane, Lynn Lott and H. Stephen Glenn. *Positive Discipline in the Classroom.* Rocklin, CA: Prima Publishing, 1997.

Oetker, Dr. *Dr. Oetker Schul-Kochbuch.* Bielefeld (DE): Ceres-Verlag, 1951.

Prokofieff, Sergej O. *Ewige Individualität. Zur karmischen Novalis-Biographie.* Dornach (CH): Verlag am Goetheanum, 1987.
Rawson, Martyn and Tobias Richter. *The Educational Tasks and Content of the Steiner Waldorf Curriculum.* Forest Row (UK): Steiner Schools Fellowship Publications, 2000.

Rehbach, Conrad. *Von Köln nach Kuwait.* Viroqua, WI: Selbstverlag, 2007.

Rilke, Rainer Maria. *Poems from the Book of Hours.* New York: New Directions Publishing Corporation, 1941.

Ritter, Heinz. *Eins und Alles. Gedichte für Kindheit und Jugend.* Stuttgart (DE): Verlag Freies Geistesleben, 1979.

Schäpers, Roland. *Deutsch 2000. Eine Einführung in die modern Umgangssprache.* München (DE): Max Hueber Verlag, 1973.

Schulz, Hans und Wilhelm Sundermeyer. *Deutsche Sprachlehre für Ausländer.* München (DE): Max Hueber Verlag, 1971.

Steiner, Rudolf. *The Education of the Child.* Hudson, NY: Anthroposophic Press, 1996.

Stöcklin-Meier, Susanne. *Sprechen und Spielen.* Ravensburg (DE): Ravensburger Buchverlag, 1995.

Stott, Michael. *Foreign Language Teaching in Rudolf Steiner Schools.* Stroud (UK): Hawthorn Press, 1995.

Szecsy, Elsie M. *German is Fun, Book 1.* New York: Amsco School Publications, 1993.

Taylor, Uta. *Deutsch als Fremdsprache in der Waldorfschule. Anregungen zu Lehrplan und Methode.* Stuttgart (DE): Pädagogische Forschungsstelle beim Bund der Freien Waldorfschulen, 2002.

Tolstoi, Leo. *Kleine Geschichten.* Berlin (DE): Kinderbuchverlag, 1966.

Von Heydebrand, Caroline. *Curriculum of the First Waldorf School.* Forest Row (UK): Steiner Schools Fellowship Publications, 1966.

Weis, Erich. *Grund- und Aufbauwortschatz Englisch.* Stuttgart (DE): Ernst Klett Verlag, 1984.

About the author:

Conrad Rehbach *earned a M. A. in Social Pedagogy at the Polytechnic University for Social Pedagogy, Berlin, Germany (1981); he is an ANSWA Certified Waldorf Teacher, having graduated from the Waldorf Teacher Training/Antioch New England Graduate School, Keene, New Hampshire, USA (1993). Conrad is the founder and director of the Sophia Institute (1998 – present), which offers Waldorf Teacher Training courses and adult education courses, including Foundation Courses in Anthroposophy and the Arts since 1998.*

Conrad has been the administrator/school coordinator and teacher of German/Math/Life Skills at the Youth Initiative High School, Viroqua, Wisconsin from 1998 – 2007. Previously, Conrad has been a Waldorf class teacher and tutor at the Camphill Village Minnesota School, a co-worker in the Camphill Movement for Curative Education and Social Therapy in the USA and Canada (1985-1997), and a social worker/counselor working with refugee

children at an orphanage in Berlin, Germany (1981-1984). Conrad's favorite artist is Wassily Kandinsky (1866—1944).